The Book Of

yoga

The Book Of
yoga

Bringing the body, mind and spirit into balance and harmony

Christina Brown

p

This is a Parragon Publishing Book
This edition published in 2004

Parragon Publishing
Queen Street House
4 Queen Street
Bath BA1 1HE, UK

Created and produced for Parragon by
THE BRIDGEWATER BOOK COMPANY LIMITED

CREATIVE DIRECTOR Stephen Knowlden
EDITORIAL DIRECTOR Fiona Biggs
PROJECT DESIGNER Alison Honey
EDITOR Nicola Wright
DESIGNER Alistair Plumb
PICTURE RESEARCH Vanessa Fletcher
PHOTOGRAPHER Colin Husband
ILLUSTRATION Michael Courtney

ISBN: 1-40543-165-2

Printed in China

The publishers wish to thank Getty Images for the use
of photographs: Steve Smith 14, V.C.L. 17, Robert Daly 27,
Michael Krasowitz 55, Antony Nagelmann 83.
Cover by 20 Twenty Design

MODELS: Christina Brown, Christiana Polites,
Carman Taylor Haywood, Cate Peterson,
Paul O'Byrne, Peter Hooker.

Dedication
To all the yogis
whose dedication keeps them
rolling out their mats
in the solitude of practice.

Contents

Part 1 Introduction to Yoga   6

Introduction   8

History and Philosophy   18

Part 2 The Practice   22

Starting The Journey   24

Yoga Relaxation   26

Building Awareness   34

Standing Postures   40

Forward Bends   54

Backbends   70

Twists   82

Balances   90

Inversions   98

Dynamic Yoga   108

Restorative Yoga   110

Yoga on a Chair   116

Structuring Your Practice   118

Part 3 Pranayama   122

Pranayama   124

About Breathing   126

Part 4 Meditation   134

Meditation   136

Mantras and Chanting   142

Part 5 The Kundalini Path   144

Chakras   146

Part 6 Therapeutic Yoga   154

Therapeutic Yoga   156

Index   160

Introduction to Yoga

Introduction

After their first yoga class, people often report that they've slept better and feel taller. Yoga has helped people lose weight, overcome fears, conquer habits like smoking, and develop better concentration, all of which help their performance in their daily tasks. Others feel improved self-awareness, a deeper sense of well-being, developed compassion, enhanced relationships, greater self-acceptance, and a sensation of being at peace.

As we nudge our physical boundaries with yoga postures, we become fully focused on the body, breath and mind. We become absorbed in being in the present moment. It's like a break from our usual mind status. Like a holiday, it refreshes us. Yoga practice helps us move from distress to de-stress, from dis-ease to ease, from passion to compassion.

Contrary to what many believe, yoga is not a set of exercises or a meditation technique. It is actually a state of mind. The state of yoga is when the mind is still.

The turnings of the thoughts have ceased and there are no distractions. This state of mind was primarily sought through the practice of meditation. Over the last two thousand years, other practices were developed that helped the body and mind become receptive to the experience of stillness. Of these practices, asana (physical postures) is the practice most commonly equated with yoga in the West.

Stillness fosters awareness. When we know we have forgotten something, we often freeze momentarily while we remember. Hatha yoga includes physical exercises that seek to relax and still the body, breath work to focus the mind, relaxation to quieten the body and mind, chanting to arouse and then calm the emotions, and meditation to center the spirit.

The word yoga originates from the Sanskrit *yuj*. Yuj may be translated as "to center one's thoughts", "to concentrate oneself" or "to meditate deeply". All of these things involve the slowing of the movements of the mind. From yuj also comes to "unite", "join" and "connect", which implies a reintegration; a bringing back into balance. It is often said that yoga means union, as it harmonizes the body, breath, mind and spirit. But, paradoxically, yoga also seeks to disunite. The spirit, considered pure and eternal, separates from the physical body that temporarily houses it, and its purity, never lost but perhaps hidden, is regained. Lastly, from the root *yuj* comes "to yoke". Yoking, or harnessing one's energies connotes effort, and the collection of Hatha yoga practices and precepts certainly require this. The codes of moral conduct, physical exercises, breathing practices, concentration and meditation all require effort, and all contribute to the goal of self-realization.

Keeping a healthy discipline makes life feel better. You feel better after you've finished a yoga practice than when you started it. Sometimes you begin your practice feeling unfocused, anxious or tight in your body. Sometimes you feel lazy and lethargic. Yet after absorbing yourself in your practice, you feel warm, loose, relaxed, calm and perhaps more connected to a force greater than you. Because it feels so good, the practice itself is your reward as well as the journey along the path.

> *Yoga is the ability to direct the mind exclusively toward an object and sustain that direction without any distractions.*
>
> YOGA-SUTRA I:2

Being off balance doesn't feel good. Teetering on the edge, being about to topple over, feels unsafe. It's difficult to relate to others in a relaxed, authentic way if you feel that the environment you have created might not survive a few storm clouds. Fear fades and tranquility arrives when you relax back into a sense of wholeness. It's like lying back in a warm bath. It's when you re-remember who you really are when, caught up in the whirlwind of life, you'd forgotten yourself for a while.

Every yoga practice is a small reversal of consciousness. With yoga we come back to ourselves to understand our essential goodness, purity and wholeness. It feels wonderful. Yoga is a metaphor for life: finding your center in a pose encourages you to find your center during the rest of your life and follow the right path for you. You might feel moved to change aspects of your life that are off kilter. It doesn't mean you become a different person, but rather that you learn more about yourself and become more authentic. It isn't always possible to anticipate the ways we will change.

Right: The ancient texts tell us that the state of yoga can be reached through dedication and practice.

Above: Yoga postures bring strength to
weak areas of the body and soften the
tight spots.

Most of us have a resistance to change, especially when
things are going wrong. But, if we are in a state of suffering,
in the long run it is always more painful not to change.
When you experience stillness and get a sense of the bigger
picture, you develop respect for your intuition and trust in
yourself. From this stems the courage to change, even
though your choice may perhaps be a rather intuitive one,
the sense and purpose of which may not always seem logical
to others.

When you practice yoga, you might spend 30 minutes
on the mat twice a week, or you might expand it out into
your way of life. When you are right there in the moment,
there is nothing to work toward, and, as you mentally sink
into that moment, your worries fall away. Yoga lets us practice
being in the present. Be here now. The reality is that the
present moment is all we really possess. Truly "having"
anything else is just an illusion. Yoga for you might be going

for a long, slow, musing walk. It could be a sense of
connection coming from watching a sunset or communing
with nature. Maybe it's dancing underwater that brings you
back to this state of union. Or it could perhaps be leaning
against a doorway or a post at the bus stop to stretch and
really feel what it's like to be in your body. It could be taking
three breaths to reconnect with yourself before answering
the phone. Why take just a sip of water when you can bathe
in it? The same could be said for the yoga in your life. Yoga
is a tremendous tool for transformation. Everyone has a
different yoga practice. I hope this book helps you find
your yoga.

The Asanas

Watching my cats wake up is a lesson in itself. They
always stretch out beautifully. They reach forward and stretch
back just like the yoga pose of Downward-Facing Dog.
Then they round their backs while arching up (which we
call Cat Pose), and yawn. Slow stretching is glorious. It feels
good and the body likes it. Our body wants to move and was
designed for it. Basically, it feels better to be loose and free
than to be all bound up, tense and contracted.

A yoga asana is a posture where you are externally still
yet internally alive. To take part in asana practice is to use
your body as the doorway through which to experience and
remember the truth about who you are. Since we have a
body we have an opportunity to use it as a tool. From the
Sanskrit *seat*, the English translation, "pose", implies that
there is a "holding", an action that requires effort and mental
presence. By holding an asana we can integrate the body,
breath and mind.

One of the most common mental blocks for a beginner
is the belief that he or she is not flexible enough for yoga.
Advanced practitioners make the action look effortless.
Many of the photos in this book are of teachers who have
many years of asana practice behind them. Mostly, the fullest
forms of the asanas are shown. This is meant to inspire you,

not discourage you. With yoga, you just start from where you are—there is no other possible place to start from! The main thing is just to start.

As long as your alignment is not harming your body, it is not important whether or not your pose looks graceful. What matters is that you find the teaching point for that pose. That point may be different for you than for another, but when two people are stretching to their personal limit, they will both be getting a similar effect. It may be that, due to your body's individuality, you need to change the posture to fit you, rather than overriding the body's needs by forcing it to conform to an 'ideal' shape. More than poise in the posture, it is the breath that should be graceful.

According to the *Yoga-Sutra*, the first codification of yoga, which dates back about 2,000 years, an asana must have the qualities of alertness and relaxation. It is perfected when no effort is necessary, hence relaxation is truly possible. Even if you feel like you have the flexibility of a block of wood at times, keep in mind the concept of *abhyasa*, "repeated effort". With repeated effort you will eventually cease to have to try. Asana practice is a frequently repeated effort made in order to reach an effortless state.

Stretching your body stretches your mind. At first it is enough to keep in mind the area of most intense stretch. Later, you can increase your awareness to include the surrounding area. The detailed instructions make your movement more deliberate. They help bring consciousness to the pose. From the toes eventually your awareness can reach the left elbow, then eventually cover the whole body.

Asanas help balance the body. They distribute strength and flexibility more evenly between left and right, top and bottom, front and back. They develop strength in weaker areas of the body, and softness in tighter spots. They make space in the body. Through freeing up the outer body, asanas

build and control the *prana*—the vital force—in the inner body. On an energetic level, polarity therapists believe the joints in the body can be weaker areas, and yoga postures mobilize and vitalize the joints. Hatha yoga is a great do-it-yourself preventive medicine. For more on the physical effects of yoga practice, see the section on yoga therapy.

Asanas with attention to correct alignment redesign the body and undo less than optimal holding patterns. In addition, as ancient spiritual shapes, they provide a work-*in*, not just a work-out. Beyond the physical realm, they alter our subtle energies. Asanas are considered purifying and healing for the body. They have psycho-spiritual effects and they influence the emotions.

Asanas focus the mind and are a way of coming back to the self. Like your body finding its center of gravity in a given position, finding just where your center is in your life is helpful. Asanas teach you that moving away from your center only creates internal conflict. Becoming stiller and therefore more aware with yoga practice helps you notice when you are moving away from your center so you have the chance to bring yourself back. Yoga lets you practice being in your still, centered point. When you develop a feeling for it, you can do this anytime, any place. Practice this joyful experience many, many times in the day.

Through yoga, the body attains attractiveness to others, beauty, firmness and unusual physical strength.

YOGA-SUTRA III:46

Use your asanas as a way to observe attunement with your body. Instead of being distracted, come back with single-minded focus to explore your being. Yoga is an open listening to, and a personal response from, your own body. It should enhance your relationship with all that makes up you. Your undivided attention and compassion make a wonderful gift to yourself.

Remind yourself often that yoga is not about twisting yourself into complicated knotted-up shapes. Doing the most difficult-looking asanas is not the goal. Mastery of a specific asana won't necessarily suddenly make you enlightened. Of the 196 aphorisms in the *Yoga-Sutra*, there are only three that refer to the yoga postures themselves. Discover the inner intelligence of your cells. Consciousness is all-pervasive. The *Yoga-Sutra* tells us, "The posture is mastered and perfect when all effort is relaxed and the mind absorbed in the infinite." When the mind is so engrossed, there is no room for distracting thoughts to arise.

The Breath

Your breath will bring your yoga alive. When you are consciously breathing, your practice can never be mechanical. Explore how it feels to move with your breath, to become your breath and to let your breath breathe you. Wait for your next breath with the attentiveness of new parents waiting for the first one from their newborn baby.

From birth to death, your breath will always be there, your partner as you move through life. Good breathing is reassuring, soothing and healing. It will bring intuition to your postures. Remember that even in the seemingly stationary poses when your body might be still on the outside, it is never stagnant. While there is breath awareness, there will be a feeling of cleansing, lightness, new energy and mental clarity. If you forget your breath then come back to an exercise where the breath and movement are clearly linked so that you feel the flow. Holding the breath dulls the flow of feeling. If your breath freezes, ease the intensity of your posture, let the rhythm into the belly and chest once more, and catch the wave of the breath when it comes.

The breath is a mirror for your mind. Breath and mind are intrinsically connected. Any alteration in one will affect the other. The mind can multiply in ways that the breath cannot. As the breath is the slower moving of the two, choosing to focus on it during asana practice will help to calm the churnings of thought. Awareness of the breath

> *Mind is the master of the senses, and the breath is the master of the mind.*
>
> HATHA YOGA PRADIPIKA IV:29

will draw your mind to the present moment. Evenness in your breath will be reflected in your mind. The breath is your monitor of how you are doing in the pose. When the breath flows steadily, your asana becomes closer to being perfected.

Your natural breath can't be created by will-power alone. You can breathe freely only through releasing and undoing. Like fingerprints, each person's breathing is unique and no two breaths will be identical. The natural breath unshrinks and unkinks us and teaches us that sometimes the most subtle methods are the most profound. Come back to the breath often throughout the day. Put notes around your home, on walls and in drawers to remind you to check in with how you are breathing.

There is freedom in yawning. Yawning is letting go. One of my students starts yawning as soon as he steps on the mat. Through the class, he yawns until tears stream down his face. He works hard in life but he knows how to release too. He loves yoga, and his practice is a wonderful reminder about letting go.

Breathe in and out through the nose so that the air is filtered and warmed. To bring constancy to your breath, practice yoga asanas with a steady, pleasant Ujjayi breath (see page 131). In general, inhale on opening or unfolding the body, when performing rising up or lengthening movements, when twisting the upper back and when bending backward. Exhale when releasing, closing the body, moving downward, twisting the lower back, lowering the arms or legs, and when bending forward or sideways. These are general rules but do experiment to intuit what feels right for your body. Try a practice moving only on the exhalation, for example. The slower you move, the more easily awareness will come. In flowing postures, such as Cat Pose (see page 37), experiment with taking three or five breaths to complete a single movement. Remind yourself that it's irrelevant whether you can touch your toes or not. If you can breathe, you can practice yoga.

Staying Present

When you stay mentally present in a pose, awareness deepens. There are two types of asanas: conscious and unconscious. In a conscious position, the quality of the asana moves from that of body conditioner to become a psycho-spiritual exercise. When you are absorbed in the subtle sensations of the body, your mind is not permitted to dance away. Allow the internal awakening to take place. Your mind will naturally run to the part of your body where the feelings are intense, but try to spread your awareness simultaneously and evenly over your body. For example from observing your hamstring in a forward bend, radiate your awareness to the whole leg, then keep radiating it out until it touches the entire body.

During your practice you create the space to have a conversation with yourself. If you like, pose a question and then wait for a response. Or don't ask anything. Just be receptive in a pose, or, when you come out of it, open to what your body wants to communicate with you that day.

Your body is your playground, your classroom, your tool for learning. If you spend one minute in a posture, observe, sense, visualize and refine. Deepen your understanding. Seek that still point, the epicenter of consciousness. Over the duration of your practice, these "one minutes" join together to create a unit of time during which you have been perfectly present. These blocks of time are healing and refreshing. They offer us a new way of being, freeing us momentarily from other concerns. In time, these small chunks of present moment focus can even extend from your practice session into your life.

Doing and Undoing

Fully engaging a muscle will bring the mind right to

Above: Finding the quietness that lies within yourself is calming, soothing and life enhancing.

that area. All-over awareness is excellent practice for concentration and being in the now. With the muscles engaged, the mind is engaged and this is why yoga asanas have transformative power.

According to the *Yoga-Sutra*, an asana needs to be steady and comfortable. The stretching of yoga aims to expand, not strain. Strain blocks your ability to listen to what the body has to tell you. Go to the deepest you can, then hold it a little bit more. Non-harming is one of the precepts of yoga philosophy, and this certainly includes your treatment of your body. Overworking your body is neglecting to take care, a form of misuse. In yoga, as in life, it is essential to keep extending your limits. Live fully by exploring your body's potential. Do this by coaxing and persuading but don't force. Frowning, clenching your jaw and holding your breath are

Left: Have fun in your practice. Your body is a playground for learning new things about yourself.

seem strange. Counter the effort of doing with plenty of undoing. Do more by doing less. Let the earth take your weight. If you are standing, enjoy the relief in surrendering your weight down through the soles of the feet. If you are sitting, sink down through the sitting bones. If you are balancing on your hands, soften the skin on the palms and release downward. This downward energy rebounds upward to be used in your posture. If the release won't come in a posture, slow rhythmic movement may help. Flow in and out of the pose several times, before finally holding the pose. As you release the air from your lungs, release the tension in the body. Don't force, simply yield with each exhalation to extend further. Let tension move out of your body.

As we move through life, we collect so many experiences. They stack up and get stored in the cellular memory of our bodies. During asana practice, you have a wonderful opportunity to explore and soften this unconscious holding on. Release the superfluous emotional overlays that hold you back. Regain the sense of freedom and peace by rediscovering your true essence.

Anchoring and Radiating

With yoga, as in life, we need a base from which to move. When we are stable and grounded, directional movement can be focused. While one part of your body is well grounded, another part can rise up. When you anchor yourself securely, it makes the exercise more of a challenge. Often, less flexible people have a better yoga practice than those who are very flexible. Stiffer-bodied people know intuitively about anchoring and working from their base. People who are naturally very flexible have to learn how to anchor themselves. Having a point from which to extend yourself is physiologically a bit like using weights in a gym. As you

signs to back off. If you notice yourself feeling competitive, smile and let go of it.

Some days it feels hard to pull yourself up out of your comfortable armchair. Other days you effortlessly spring up. When you engage the mind in the posture, you give strength to the posture. With strength comes a lovely feeling of lightness too. It's like changing from a heavy, old car to a brand new one with power steering. When you have energy, strength and lightness, it's much more pleasurable to move your body around.

Upon first meeting a posture it might feel that it requires one hundred percent effort to hold it. It can be hard to imagine being able to find any release in the pose at all. As you practice and become more comfortable with the pose, the effort required slowly reduces. Some space develops and you can release into it. With time and dedication, the proportion of doing to undoing will slide. The asana will feel more comfortable and more rewarding. Freedom comes into the pose.

We are accustomed to the concept of using effort to get somewhere. Letting go in order to achieve something might engage your muscles, there is a point from which to work.

Consider where your anchor is in each pose. The floor acts as your base when standing. As you take your arms overhead, extend and radiate upward from floor to fingertips. When you sit to bend forward, ground down through the sitting bones. When you lie prone to backbend, press down through the pubic bone and radiate out from the lower abdomen. When you sit to twist right, anchor the left buttock well down. In Shoulderstand, let the shoulders and elbows be heavy so the rest of the body can float lightly upward. When your hold your arms horizontal and stretch them apart, radiate your energy along the arms and reach outward, so it feels like it is not just your muscular power holding them in place, but your mental energy stretching them away.

An integral being knows without going, sees without looking and accomplishes without doing.

LAO TZU

Our center of gravity lies 2in (5cm) below the navel. Learn to move from this center. This core acts as an anchor from which to extend. Then the movement from the center to the extremities feels integrated, and ripples of energy flow from our center to the rest of the body. Link them with the breath, the extension outward and gentle rebounding flow back. Practice extending yourself without losing yourself. The earth supports us, shelters us, feeds us, yet sometimes we lose our sense of connection with it. Re-center, and extend to your limit while maintaining constant awareness of what is always there to support you.

Bandhas

A bandha is a kind of mudra (see page 138). It involves the contraction of certain muscles to unlock the pranic vital energies so it can be directed upward. Bandhas may be used in conjunction with pranayama or asana practice to encourage the flow of the vital force and preserve it.

The bandhas are very useful during asana practice. They work with the organs, and the nervous and endocrine systems. They can improve disorders of the reproductive and urinary systems, sexual dysfunction and back problems, and are helpful after childbirth.

The mulabandha is located at the perineum—the area between the anus and the genitals, and about 1in (2.5cm) in toward the core of the body. For women, it is also linked to the cervix. Uddhyanabandha is located in the core of the body just below the navel.

To practice with mulabandha and uddhyanabandha, sit erect. On your next inhalation, draw in the lower abdomen—the part just above the pubic bone and below the navel. As you do this, the perineum will lift slightly and a gentle mulabandha holding will be activated. Move between drawing in on the inhalation and letting go on the exhalation, so you get a sense of lifting in the pelvis.

When you are not used to isolating the mulabandha area, the surrounding muscles seem to want to tense up in sympathy. You might find your buttocks, thighs and anus tightening, or that you are unconsciously holding your breath. In time, you will be able to more actively draw up the perineum without tensing other muscles.

The bandhas respond to different parts of the breath—while drawing in the lower abdomen is easiest on the inhalation, you might notice that actively drawing up the perineum feels easiest on an exhalation. Practice this while sitting, then begin to incorporate it into forward bends and standing poses. Eventually bring it into the other poses too.

Discomfort and Pain

During your practice you will feel intense sensations. The sensations you get from a strong stretch are not necessarily bad. You might feel discomfort, which is a "good hurt", or pain, a negative hurt. Discomfort is resistance of the body or mind. When exploring new territory, mental and physical unease will inevitably arise.

Pain is more acute than discomfort. Discomfort, when caused by working strongly, is a positive feeling. With pain, there will be nothing pleasant about the soreness. Pain in a pose means that you have overshot your limit by moving too quickly, or that you are improperly aligned. Pain is counterproductive as the body will instinctively tense and move away from it. Pain in the muscles or joints could lead to injury so never ignore it. Come out of the pose and examine your alignment or check with a teacher.

A high strain will force your attention away, while, if you are underworking your body, the mind will become lethargic. Optimum strain, working just at your edge, will engage your mind. When your body experiences a healthy amount of tension, you can move internally and tune into the quietness. Remember that yoga seeks to remove pain and suffering, not increase it. Your practice should bring joy.

Your Edge

Your edge is the point at which the strong challenge comes into the pose and where you feel you have reached a new frontier. During practice, aim to push back your edge in a slow and respectful way. Take time to listen to your body's feedback, not only immediately after practice but over the following days. Each pose has many edges; each one is a point of learning, an opportunity to grow. As you approach your first edge, hold the position with a steady breath. Stay focused on that place in your body. The exhalation will help soften and prepare the body to move beyond it. Wait for your body to let you in. Should that inner cue come, proceed respectfully, with full attention. Then you have found a new edge. Likewise, it is good to be adventurous but this does not mean being aggressive.

Just where your edge is varies from breath to breath, practice to practice, day to day. Rediscover your limit in every pose. Never take it for granted that you can stretch as far as you did yesterday. Never assume that you can't because you couldn't before.

Right: While keeping in mind your intent, stay open to whatever arises. Apart from a wished-for end point, your practice is a reward in itself.

It's irrelevant where your edge is in an asana. It is unimportant how far you stretch before you find it. Whether you reach your fingertips to your knees as you fold forward or whether you easily grasp your feet, let go of preconceptions of "good" or "proper" yoga. Seek instead just to find the point where you can learn about yourself, explore and grow.

Your psychological edge might be different to your physical edge. Respect both. Yoga should help you deal with life, not hinder the process. Yoga asanas are a controlled means of exposing yourself to a difficult situation. They are meant to challenge you. They offer practice at mastering your reaction under stressful conditions. If you experience mental unease, absorb yourself in the breath. Should you find you are in a place that feels wrong, change it. If either your body or mind is telling you "no", don't push past it. Instead, as you do whenever circumstances change in your life, adjust. Be mentally flexible too. Sensitively encourage yourself using your breath, but never force it. Forcing will just introduce fear. Yoga teaches compassion for all living beings, and that includes yourself.

Your Intention

Consider what you want to achieve with yoga. You might want to increase your strength or flexibility, heal an ailment, find better body awareness, cope with stress, find inner peace, develop compassion or explore your spirituality. Write down what it is you want so that you will be clear and can form your practice around your goal. Also write how much time you can realistically expect to practice.

Yoga is not religious. Though yoga has been embraced by Hinduism, as they are both from Indian soil, there is nothing in the yoga texts that speaks of Hinduism.

The writings do, however, recognize a divine principle, a universal energy. If you have a religious tradition that you find helpful, then keep your personal god in mind. If not, consider your higher goals, or ideals that inspire you and that you would like to embody. Keeping an energy greater than ourselves in mind fosters our ability to attune to our higher self. Communing to the bigger picture shrinks our concerns away. It teaches us that we are not islands. Nothing exists in isolation. It gives us a sense of being not separate from, but instead supported by, something wiser than ourselves.

At the start of your practice you might like to light a candle or a stick of incense, offer a chant or prayer, or repeat an affirmation. Or you might look at a picture of your personal god, or a photo of someone inspirational who has qualities you admire. Take some time at the beginning to sit or lie quietly and access the stillness within. Be clear of your intent, but begin each practice with an open mind. Yoga, stilling the fluctuations of the mind, is an endpoint, but your practice is part of your journey, and a reward in itself.

Be clear that this is time for you alone. Close the door and turn off the phones. Let others know not to distract you. Your practice is a reflection of your life. Delight in it.

When a posture feels cumbersome and heavy, it will be less enjoyable. Bring mental lightness to your practice too. Enthusiasm always lightens the load. Don't let yourself become mentally lazy. Question yourself always. Practice with renewed effort when you feel lazy. If you feel you are a Type A over-achiever, learn to ease off when your body requires it. Work honestly, with integrity, curiosity and enthusiasm. I often wonder about those on a spiritual path who never seem to laugh. Playfulness leads to new discoveries. Be joyful in your practice.

History and Philosophy

Hatha yoga consists of eight limbs of practices. They are not steps to be worked on one by one, but branches that can be explored many at a time.

1 The Yamas

The first limb consists of the yamas, which guide us in how we relate to others, our actions, thoughts and speech. There are five listed in the *Yoga-Sutra*:

Ahimsa—Consideration for All Living Things

Often ahimsa is translated as non-violence or non-injury, but, more fully, this yama encompasses compassion for all beings. Under the precept of ahimsa, we avoid causing unnecessary pain to others. Most people think first of things like refraining from killing insects or being abusive to others. However this precept includes more subtle things such as restraining yourself from gossip and mastering your negative thoughts toward the person who cuts in front of you in the supermarket. It means refraining from raising your voice, and examining yourself carefully when criticizing others so that

you do it in a positive way. Ahimsa also encompasses protecting the environment for others by treating nature respectfully and recycling used materials. Under ahimsa, develop qualities of kindness, patience and tolerance, not just for others but for yourself too. Choose kind thoughts over unkind thoughts. Direct compassionate thoughts toward yourself even when you consider you have failed. Next time you look in the mirror and catch yourself criticizing your appearance, replace those self-harming thoughts with positive ones. Incorporate ahimsa in the way you eat. Choose foods that will nourish you properly.

Satya—Right Communication

Satya deals with truthfulness. Aside from not telling outright lies, satya encompasses honesty in behavior and thought. It means restraining from deceptions such as embellishing stories. It means refusing to make a promise you don't think you can keep. Next time you are tempted to tell a "white" lie, be honest with yourself about your motivation. Is it to protect another, or is it due to your laziness or inability to face an uncomfortable situation?

Lack of truth in any relationship, whether it be with ourselves or another, doesn't work to build a stable foundation. In the many layers of consciousness, it is difficult to avoid lying to ourselves sometimes. Our task is to approach life with integrity and sincerity. Do your best and have faith that with time you will achieve clarity.

Truthfulness in behavior provides still another set of challenges. Behave in accordance with your own truths. Living according to satya is certainly not always convenient. It means deciding what you do thoughtfully. The thing you spend so many hours at each week, your job, needs to be chosen very carefully. Seek your dharma—what it is that you can offer to the world, what you can do best, and incorporate it in your life.

Asteya—Non-Covetousness

Asteya means much more than its frequent translation as non-stealing. It's also about resisting the desire for much that doesn't belong to us. Unless we rein in these desires, we risk living in a constant state of unfulfilled wanting, which just keeps on spiralling. Yoga teaches detachment from material possessions. Enjoy the simpler gifts of life.

Asteya includes not taking that which is not freely given. This may include not stealing another person's time by being late, or not bullying someone into providing you with something you want. It includes not claiming welfare when you already have a job, or lying on your tax return. It means not burning your own copies of a CD thus depriving the artist of their royalties, or "taking" the husband or wife of another in an extramarital affair. Asteya encompasses giving credit where it is due and not taking another's ideas without acknowledgement.

Brahmacharya—Moderation in Our Actions

Brahmacharya has many levels of interpretation, one of which is celibacy. Many spiritual traditions preach celibacy, not because they consider that sex is inherently bad, but so that energies remain contained and can be used instead to uplift the Self.

Celibacy as a tool for discovering oneself can be a joyous, self-nurturing and educational experience. When it is approached with rigid and joyless determination, emotions can become suppressed, backfire and cause suffering. An appropriate interpretation of brahmacharya for a Westerner might be being more moderate in thoughts and actions and not indulging the senses above all else. Channelling your sexuality with thought and care helps you respect its power and enables you to use it with love rather than in a harmful way. It means distinguishing between sex and love and refraining from inappropriate behavior like flirting or game playing in relationships. To consider how far-reaching this is, consider chastity not only of action, but of speech and thought.

The unifying force of sex with love is similar to the uplifting merging with God. Brahmacharya encompasses merging with the Divine. This is a much bigger commitment than merely adopting sexual chastity. As for a priest or nun, brahmacharya involves a marriage-like commitment to the union with God.

Aparigraha—Non-Greediness

Aparigraha prompts you to consider your true needs. First you need to determine what is a true need, and what is merely a desire or a want. Quite simply, the less you need, the greater chance you have of being happy. While we stay attached to things we can only be unhappy, as their loss would cause us pain. Let go of the urge to accumulate. Don't let what you have be your yardstick of success. Practice simplicity by paring down your material possessions to the essentials.

Under aparigraha, we seek to reduce our constant desires for more and are able to take only what is appropriate. It's a habit that begins in the mind. When you reach for more less often, you start to downsize the spiral of want. Instead of grasping, enjoy what you already have. Rather than clingingly making plans to get what you want, consider how easily you give to others. You may be lucky enough to know someone who is materially poor, yet has a joyful and rich life. Let that person inspire you. Don't hang your happiness on external things. Appreciate that which is around you—sunshine, healthy food, fresh air, your health, uplifting conversation, a good friend.

2 The Niyamas

The second limb, niyamas, deals with our attitudes toward ourselves. The *Yoga-Sutra* lists five:

Saucha—Purity

Saucha is cleanliness of your physical body and surroundings. As the mind and body influence each other so much, a wholesome diet contributes to purity of the mind. Purity in your environment means not cluttering your living space with material possessions. Cleanliness of living encompasses what you say, read and watch on TV, and who you choose to associate with.

Yoga cleanses the body with postures and breathing techniques. Clearing the mind through observance of the yamas and niyamas, and cleansing the spirit with practices like meditation, allows for clarity of thinking.

Santosha—Contentment

With santosha we cultivate being satisfied with what we have. Practice being comfortable with that which you do have, whether it be the knowledge that your basic needs are met, wonderful memories, your friendships or your health. Appreciating these things goes a long way toward giving us the happiness we seek. Cultivating santosha also encompasses adopting an uncomplaining, cheerful and comfortable approach toward what you don't have.

Should you find yourself in a difficult situation, seek to live with it in the best possible way. Santosha does not involve accepting what you have because you are too lazy to put in the effort to change it. Rather than choosing to be passive about a situation because it is easier to stay in a rut and escape from your responsibilities to yourself, continue to cultivate inner growth. Even while you work to change any difficult situation, have patience, trust and hope that it will change for the better.

Tapas—Burning Enthusiasm

Tap means to burn or to cook. Under the precept of tapas, you cook the raw ingredients of which you are composed to produce a beautiful dish. Tapas involves the self-control to live with right action; good habits in all things including work, food, drink, spirituality, thoughts and wishes. For some, tapas may involve purificatory practices like periodic fasting or regularly observing silence.

Tapas also means fire. With strong resolve our energies give us momentum to do the work that needs to be done. Bring enthusiasm to your practice and to your life, even to the most ordinary-seeming parts of your life. Tapas encompasses the self-discipline of staying focused on your spiritual path. You will move in the direction in which you are looking. When you concentrate on your goals, you will move closer to them. Persist and don't give up too soon.

Swadhyaya—Self-Study

Self-discovery demands a turning of the attention inward. With alertness and curiosity, observe your responses under all circumstances. Whether you are relaxed or stressed, happy or sad, full or empty, busy or unoccupied, practice mindful self-reflection. Many people find keeping a journal helpful as a way of evaluating their progress. Some choose therapy on their path to self-discovery; others attend classes, workshops or spiritual lectures. Read uplifting literature and other yoga books. You might start with the modern yoga books, which feel easier to digest. Classic yoga texts are the *Yoga-Sutra* and the *Hatha Yoga Pradipika*. Many people enjoy the *Bhagavad-Gita*, a Hindu classic. As well as drawing your attention inward, do explore the outer world too. Extend your mind with philosophy and other studies that help you understand the world in which you participate.

Ishvarapranidhana—Celebration of the Spiritual

Under this precept we accept the existence of a higher intelligence. By honouring our relation to this all-knowing principle we can surrender our small ego before a higher will. By releasing our personal will to a greater intelligence, we can be helped to fulfil our destiny. Under ishvarapranidhana, remember too that there is no separation between you and this omnipresent force. It is not merely external, but it lies always within. Using ritual helps bring meaning to your life. It is a reminder of a higher intelligence. If you don't have a personal god, your interpretation of ishvarapranidhana may be to celebrate an ideal.

3 Asana—Postures

Asana, the third limb of yoga, is using physical postures as a method of self-study and exploration. Asana prepares the body and mind for meditation. (See the asana section on page 22.)

4 Pranayama—Control of the Prana

While the breath comes automatically and unconsciously, pranayama is the conscious, deliberate regulation of the breath and prana, the vital force. (See the pranayama section on page 122.)

5 Pratyahara—Withdrawal of the Senses

A good example of pratyahara is when your hearing switches off from the dripping of a faucet because you are so engrossed in reading a good book. The senses are wonderful tools for relating to the world. They offer us rich experiences, but, at the same time, distract us from looking at the riches within. While the senses are outward looking, self-discovery involves turning the attention inward. Often we are at the mercy of the senses. Rather than the mind controlling the senses, their cravings for satisfaction control the mind. With pratyahara we seek to subdue the senses. By reducing external stimulation we withdraw to explore that which is internal. When we need to access something in the brain, we might close our eyes to quieten the senses.

Practice pratyahara by listening to less radio and watching less TV. Practice deep relaxation and meditation. Starting with short pratyahara practices will give your mind practice at gradually losing interest in what the senses have to say. Then pratyahara comes more naturally.

6 Dharana—Concentration

To maintain a mind undisturbed in its focus requires a certain mastery of it. As with all big tasks, this idea of perfect mental focus can be daunting. Start small. Divide your dharana practice into small blocks of time—perhaps 30 seconds in an asana when you direct your mind to your body. During pranayama, direct it exclusively to the breath. Just as with any physical exercise, by practicing this mental exercise you will become more accomplished in time.

7 Dhyana—Meditation

Dhyana is a one-pointed mental focus around a single subject. (See the meditation section on page 134.)

8 Samadhi—Bliss State

This is the highest level of experience and the goal of yoga, a bliss-state where there is a sense of oneness, a connection to the Absolute. The yogi reconnects with his or her essential purity yet personal identity is not lost. The mind is mastered and all thoughts are stilled in this illuminated trance-like state.

Part 2

The Practice

Starting the Journey

The following guidelines will help you

get more out of your practice.

Creating a special yoga practice area will reaffirm your commitment. You don't need much space, but make sure the area is warm, clean and uncluttered. Choose non-restrictive clothes that you feel good in. Dress in layers to remain comfortable throughout your practice. Bare feet are best—wear socks only when your feet are cold. Intense practice in direct sunlight tends to be fatiguing, but relaxing in its warmth at the end is lovely. Practicing outside lets you commune with nature, but it can be more distracting than staying inside. It's a great idea to invest in a yoga mat. Apart from providing cushioning and a non-slip surface, it will make your mental commitment to your practice stronger. You will feel you can create a yoga space anywhere, simply by rolling out your mat.

Yoga works with prana, the vital force. Asana and pranayama practice bring this energy to the cells so that they receive nourishment, and can perform their functions and heal. When you eat, your energies are made available to the digestive system in preference to the other systems. So after a meal, leave a space before you practice. Wait one hour after having a piece of fruit or a juice. Wait three or four hours after a large meal. Hydrate yourself beforehand so you don't disturb yourself during the practice.

Be realistic when you decide how much time you would like to and are able to dedicate to your practice. It is helpful to make a mental commitment. Do your best to stick to it, but don't think unkindly about yourself if you take a break. There has never been a yoga mat that has laid a guilt trip on someone who didn't use it for a while! Just work from where you are today. When you are short of time, practicing fewer poses with complete attention is preferable to rushing through many poses. From time to time, look through the book to check on the exercises you might have been avoiding. Try to embrace them into your practice bit by bit.

Left: Avoid practicing on a full stomach. Wait several hours after a large meal.

You don't need three-hour-long sessions of complicated asanas to practice "real" yoga. Sometimes one instant or a single breath is all you need to reconnect with yourself. Yoga practice is more than what you do on the mat. It is about how you live your life once you step off it, and that's 24 hours a day.

There are thousands of variations on hundreds of yoga poses but don't let this intimidate you. Even if you feel like a human ironing board, you can benefit enormously from about 20 poses practiced regularly. It's like tending a garden. Left uncared for, the soil starts to dry up and the plants start to wither. Once the garden has gotten to a certain state, it's too late to rush in with the big hoses. Large amounts of water might be more than it can readily accept, and instead it needs the kindness of water given little and often. If you have neglected your internal garden for a while, you'll need to practice in small, regular doses for it to grow and thrive.

Rather than focus on "perfecting" a posture as your measure of success in yoga, enjoy discovering your body and mind. Yoga is like life. It's a journey. Every yoga practice you have will be different, as you respond to internal and external conditions. Your thoughts change in a fraction of a second. The breath alters from second to second. How far you can stretch or hold a pose changes from minute to minute.

Empty your mind so that you can fully absorb the lessons of your practice. You never can predict just what they will be. If you are more adept, don't assume because you have practiced a posture a hundred times that you know everything about it. Keep the mind receptive and open to learning. Don't be impatient in your practice. Practice peacefully.

Keep your mind sensitive. Overstraining the body will lessen your mental sensitivity. Some days you just might not feel like getting on your mat or doing breath work. Instead, your yoga practice might include reading something spiritually uplifting.

Take things easy during menstruation. It's a special time when it is nice to allow your energies to go inside. Avoid strong backbends and strong twists. Inverted postures make the flow have to work against gravity so avoid them. Women have a natural body clock that reminds them to practice slow, restful yoga regularly, but in my classes, men are allowed to "menstruate" too! See the restorative yoga and therapeutic yoga sections (see pages 110 and 154) for more information.

While yoga has helped the pregnancies and labors of countless women, it is not safe to begin during the first three months of pregnancy. Many poses need to be modified so it's best to attend specialized classes during the second and third trimesters. See the section on therapeutic yoga for more information.

If you are suffering from any kind of health condition or have an injury, seek guidance from an experienced yoga teacher or yoga therapist. Don't practice asanas or pranayama if you have a fever.

Attend some yoga classes. Yoga is so personal that each teacher will have something different to offer you. Teachers can give valuable feedback on your alignment and ideas for practice. Try teachers from several different traditions of yoga to find which kind suits you best. Most yoga schools offer beginners' courses.

Yoga Relaxation

Center yourself with a short relaxation before starting your asana practice, and always use it at the end of your practice. The final relaxation allows your body to integrate and consolidate the effects of the poses you have been doing.

Imagine driving your car along the highway at 80 miles per hour, for weeks on end. What would happen if you stopped only briefly to check the oil and water and refill the fuel? How long would your car last if subjected to days, weeks and years of this? Now consider how you are driving your body. Like your car, your body will run better if given high-quality fuel and regular tune-ups. It will perform better for you when allowed to cool down with regular rest breaks.

Yoga asanas stir up the subtle energies (prana) of the body and the relaxation is the time that allows the prana to be directed to healing and re-energizing the system. You might feel like nothing is happening and be tempted to skip this stage, but the final relaxation is hugely important and one risks losing valuable prana by missing it. Yoga relaxation allows you to emerge refreshed and brings your body, mind and spirit back into balance. It is great after a long day or while recovering from illness. Taking 20 minutes of conscious rest is enormously effective whenever you feel tired but need to keep working.

Many students gleefully exclaim 'sleep!' when relaxation time, yoga nidra, rolls around. Indeed, yoga nidra can be translated as yogic sleep, but remember that it is a conscious rest, requiring discipline. You practice being awake yet free of body tension. After a strong session where you have really explored your boundaries, this active undoing comes easier. As you take a break from external movement, cease fidgeting and lie perfectly still, the mind becomes acutely sensitive. While you progressively let go of tension in the muscles, bones, organs, even the brain, you remain aware of the internal sensations. Whenever your thoughts stray, bring them back to your body. As the senses quieten and attention is turned inward, there is a heightened awareness. Quietening the body and mind, drawing the senses inward and accessing your inner peace are steps along the path to meditation.

Lying still with your eyes closed looks easy. But if you tend to move through life at a frenetic pace, never ceasing to stop and take stock, falling into quietness can seem difficult. Conscious relaxation is an exercise in yielding. So many of us cling tenaciously to objects, people, habits or attitudes. The principal of detachment is fundamental to Eastern philosophies. While you remain strongly attached to things, their loss will inevitably cause suffering. If you observe yourself holding onto things and accumulating material possessions, use yoga relaxation consciously to practice letting go. Physically and mentally permit yourself to release that grip and be just you, nothing else, lying on the floor. As you actively undo, you let your defenses down and accept the sense of vulnerability inherent in allowing surrender.

Try making a fist with one hand and keeping it clenched for 10 seconds. Now relax the fist and compare the feelings in the two hands. Most likely you'll feel more sensations in the hand that was clenched. As you seek to find the edge in each posture, you will be fully occupying both muscles and mind. Once the tension is released, a lingering awareness remains. The same principle applies in yoga relaxation. When you have extended your body to its limit, you'll notice how your awareness of internal sensations deepens because your mind has been completely engrossed in your practice. It will very easily let go into deep relaxation.

If you suffer from depression or phobias, don't practice Savasana but use restorative postures (see page 110) instead.

Below: Notice how as your body settles into yoga relaxation, a feeling of expansion pervades.

Getting Comfortable for Relaxation

Help yourself let go by becoming perfectly physically comfortable. Any of these modifications to the basic supine position may be helpful. See page 32 for how to make a breathing bed. Child Pose (see page 29) is useful whenever you need to relax during your practice or throughout your day, as are Makrasana (see page 114), Viparita Karani (see page 113) or Supta Konasana (see page 111).

Using a Pillow
Find the best position for your head by having a friend observe you as you lie on your back. Ideally, your chin and forehead will be at an equal height from the floor. If your chin is higher than your forehead the back of the neck will tend to shorten. Many people don't need more than a thinly folded blanket to soften the floor for the head. However, if you find your chin juts up higher than your forehead when you are lying, make a pillow.

If the forehead is too high, the throat will feel constricted. Use a folded blanket to bring your chin and forehead level.

Making a Neck Pillow
Fold a blanket three times and roll it up about halfway. Wedge this securely under your neck, right up to shoulder level. Experiment with the amount of roll. Your neck should feel very snug with the roll supporting its natural curve. Usually the chin juts out a little. If this is so fold the remaining flap down to cushion and lift the back of the head.

Supporting the Lower Back

This support lets the lower back soften down closer to the floor, and those with lower back problems find it useful. Place large rolled cushions or a bolster under your knees, and do a small pelvic tilt to flatten the lower back toward the floor. Your lower back will still curve up away from the floor, but as you then lie and let go, you will feel it ease out and release a little. If you don't have any props, then bend your knees up, place your feet just wider than body width, and lean the knees in together.

Balasana—*Child Pose*

Sit on your heels with your knees together. Fold forward over your thighs. Rest your forehead to the floor and drape your arms around you. Close your eyes and let go of any tension. Enjoy the reassuring massage of the belly pressing down into the thighs with each inhalation. For high blood pressure, or if your buttocks stay high in the air and you feel like you are nosediving, rest the forehead on a pad of folded blankets. Alternatively stack your fists one on top of the other to rest your forehead on.

COVER UP

When you relax deeply, your body temperature drops dramatically. It is impossible to completely let go when you are cold. Unless it is the height of summer, cover your whole body with a shawl or blanket.

Guided Relaxation in Savasana—*Corpse Pose*

While this pose looks like the easiest of all the yoga asanas, it is actually one of the hardest to master. While the body lets go, the mind must stay alert, observing the relaxation process, before finally surrendering into rest. The final relaxation allows your body to settle and the effects of your Hatha yoga practice to consolidate. Spend about five minutes working through the body to exaggerate the tension in your muscles, section by section. This raises the level of awareness so you can better surrender into complete relaxation. A nice way to practice Savasana is to make a tape of these instructions, with plenty of pauses, or have a friend read them aloud.

1 Lie on your back in Savasana. Your legs are apart with feet rolling out to the sides. Your arms are just out from your sides. Have the backs of your hands on the floor so your fingers curl softly up. Close your eyes so attention is drawn inward and you become sensitized to your inner environment.

2 Scrunch your toes and flex your feet. Next, spread out your toes and point the feet strongly. Then relax your feet.

3 Lift your right leg 2in (5cm) in the air. Briefly tense all the muscles in that leg and then release them, letting the leg fall to the floor. Do the same with the left leg.

4 Clench your buttocks for a few seconds so your hips rise up slightly. Release. Feel the heaviness of your lower body.

5 Tighten the muscles along the length of the spine and press the tips of your shoulders into the floor. Puff your chest up and tighten

your abdominal muscles. Then exhale and relax the muscles, let the chest release down and allow the tension to flow out of the body.

6 Lift one arm 2in (5cm) off the ground. Tighten all its muscles, make a fist with your hand, then stretch the fingers out. When you exhale let all the tension go so the arm drops back down on the floor. Repeat on the other side.

7 Lift the shoulders to the ears into a shrug and then release them back down and toward the hips.

EXPLORE

As a general rule, for every 30 minutes of asana practice, practice at least 5 minutes of Savasana. For a 90-minute practice, allow 15 minutes of relaxation at the end. But you don't need to practice any asanas to reward yourself with Savasana. Practice relaxation whenever you feel tired. Instead of taking a daytime nap, refresh with 20 minutes of Savasana.

8 Tighten all the facial muscles. Lose your inhibitions—no one is watching you! Clench your jaw muscles, squeeze the eyes tightly shut and frown. Then widen everything out and apart. Open your eyes and roll the eyeballs back, open your mouth and stick the tongue as far out toward the chin as you can. Finally, exhale with a sigh and relax the face. Feel all the skin on the face soften and any wrinkles smoothe out.

9 This time without tensing, gently drop your right ear to the floor. Take a few long breaths and become aware of the stretch on the left side of the neck. Inhale the head to the center and drop the left ear to the floor for a few breaths before bringing the head to center again.

10 Press the chin to the throat so you feel the back of the neck lengthening, then release it by softening all the neck muscles. So that you can commit to lying perfectly still for the next 10 minutes, mentally check your position and adjust anything you need to. Just as during meditation, any outer movement will distract you from your inner world.

11 Become aware of the whole body being heavy and relaxed. Your body wants to be comfortable. It is its natural state. The bones feel heavy. All the muscles are relaxed. The internal organs are free of tension. Even the tongue is relaxed. As the body releases and feels heavier, the breath lightens and feels more delicate. The brain surrenders any worries and is content, enjoying this peaceful and tranquil moment. Give permission for your emotional body to let go too. While the body relaxes, the mind stays present, observing. Finally, completely stop trying to "do". Let go of any psychological effort at all. Now rest.

12 You will intuitively know when it's time to come out of the relaxation. Begin to move the fingers and toes as you focus back on the body. Take your arms overhead along the floor and stretch up through the body, enlivening everything from fingertips to toes. When you are ready, roll over onto your side and allow the eyes to open in their own time.

EXPLORE

Your tongue is a huge muscle, attaching deep into the throat. There's much more of it than you can see when you stick it out. It usually sits touching the roof of the mouth. Instead, release it down so it floats in the center of the mouth. This relaxes the whole mouth, throat area and face. Observe whether this allows other more distant parts of the body to release too.

Revitalizing Relaxation

To make a breathing bed, fold one to three blankets so they are 8in (20cm) wide and longer than your torso. Lie over them with your buttocks on the floor and legs a little apart. The more blankets you use, the more the chest will feel it is opening, so experiment with what feels best for you. Use another blanket as a pillow so that the head is higher than the chest. Take your legs apart and let your arms rest out to the sides.

Lie on your back and lift your head for a moment to look down your body to make sure that you are perfectly symmetrical. After checking that you feel completely comfortable, begin to breathe deeply and rhythmically. As you inhale, visualize prana being drawn in through the nostrils down to your solar plexus. As you exhale it swirls around your center. With each inhalation, draw this pranic energy down to the solar plexus so that it spirals around filling up the whole torso. Each long, deep inhalation draws in more prana. While you are giving yourself the gift of vibrant energy, remember to keep the exhalations slow and steady. The full exhalation empties the lungs, allowing you to inhale this revitalizing force deeply and consciously.

From the center of the torso the spiral enlarges to cover the whole body. The outer part of the spiral reaches to circle over the head, fingertips and toes. Let yourself become the breath. With this positive energy you become enthusiastic about life and your tasks. You gain the energy to fulfil them. Stay here as long as you feel you need to.

When it is time to awaken, start moving your body and stretch a little. Feel so revitalized that the eyes blink open by themselves, as if powered by the energy within.

WHITE LIGHT

To stay true to your inner self and protect yourself from being harmed or feeling drained by others, visualize yourself surrounded with glowing white light.

Healing Visualization

The use of color is a therapeutic branch on its own. White light gives strength of spirit, clarity and protection. Black, the absence of light, brings qualities of strength, power, evolution and transition. Yellow, the color of the intellect, is uplifting and joyful. Red fosters courage, warmth and assertiveness. Orange is used for creativity, optimism and tolerance. Sky blue is linked to sincerity, peace, honesty and organizational abilities. Indigo promotes mental calmness and lessens attachment to material possessions. Violet fosters self-esteem and confidence, and dissolves the ego. Emerald green brings physical and emotional harmony and is recharging. Each chakra (see page 147) has a related color.

Choose a color to which to you feel intuitively drawn. As you lie quietly in Savasana, draw this color into any area of your body you would like to heal. With each inhalation, the color becomes clearer and brighter. It forms a dense core and, from there, begins to expand outward. In your mind's eye, visualize it expanding to fill the whole body: see it clearly filling your heart, a center for healing and unconditional love keeps enlarging it. Take several minutes, allowing it to spill over to fill the whole body all the way down the legs to the toes, and all the way down the arms to the fingertips. Breathe this color up into your head. It fills your brain, the backs of your eyes, all the crevices behind the face. You happily accept the healing energy your special color offers. You may also like to send good will or healing to loved ones. Before you complete this exercise, mentally seal your color and its particular healing qualities in your body.

Creating a Sanctuary

Think of a place where you know you can feel completely at ease. It could be a real place you have visited or seen or else an imaginary paradise—a special sanctuary where you feel completely

safe, protected and nurtured. It might be next to a still, deep pond, near the ocean, in a lush green forest or by a flickering fireplace in a wonderful home. Now, as you lie in Savasana, visualize yourself from above. From lying on the floor, visualize your body coming up to standing, and start on a pleasant trip toward your special place. Feel the sun on your skin and the breeze in your hair. Listen to the call of the birds and the other sounds around like leaves in the gentle wind or a babbling brook. In time, you arrive at your special place and settle yourself down to sit in a meditative position. Visualize yourself sitting with eyes closed and peaceful mind. Your sanctuary gives you nourishment, and you are safe there to relax completely. Continue to see yourself sitting quietly. Know that your sanctuary is always there whenever you need it. You just need to take the time to access it.

When it is time to come back, rouse yourself from sitting and take the journey back to where you are lying, until you can see yourself on the floor again. Begin to tune in to the sounds around you once again. Feel the touch of the clothes on your skin, then roll over and sit up slowly.

EXPLORE

Often mental anxiety around a health problem builds up. This creates more tension and pain. Practice directing calm, focused, accepting thoughts to that area. If only for a short time, separate yourself from your usual response to this challenge. Empty yourself of anxiety. Mentally send your breath to the area to release, soothe and heal.

Building
Awareness

The following exercises are good ways

to reconnect with yourself at the start

of a practice session.

Absorb Yourself in Your Breath

The stresses of day-to-day life can create different layers of breathing over our free, natural breath. This exercise will help you reconnect with your natural breath. Keep it simple. You are not aiming to go anywhere. You don't have to "do" anything. This is not a new technique, but rather a process of undoing. There is no need for effort, pushing or wanting. There is no search to attain the "perfect" breath. Instead, let it unravel. Often we are guided by our mental intelligence but, instead, let your instinctual natural physical intelligence take over as you unravel. Your body is what is breathing, not your mind. Your mind, relinquishing control, learns to move out of the way and becomes merely the accepting observer. Come back to this breathing exercise regularly. Make sure that you allow 20 minutes for it each time.

Lie on your back with your knees bent and feet flat on the floor. Swivel your feet so your big toes are closer together than your inner heels, then lean your knees in together so that holding them in place is effortless. Have your arms out by your sides, palms facing down. Close your eyes. Give your full attention to your breathing. Can you feel where the breath originates? Observe which part of your body moves first as you breathe in. What happens next? Observe the sequence of your body's movement when you inhale. Feel what happens to the lower and upper abdomen. How do the rib cage and chest work? Can you feel anything happening at the back? What happens to the shoulders, throat, face and nostrils? Does anything change at the pelvis?

Absorb yourself completely in your breath. You are your breath and your breath is you. It rises and falls with the rhythm of ocean waves. How do you accept your inhalation?

How do you feel the expansion? Now turn your attention to the out breath. From where do you exhale? Which part of the body begins the movement? Where does your exhalation end? Are the movements in the torso as clearly demarcated when you exhale as in your inhalation? Can you feel a consolidation of energy? Accept the support of the earth with each breath. Don't shrink, but let yourself sink.

Count the length of your in and out breaths. Which is longer? Does one come more easily to you? Become aware of the quality of your breath. Is it shallow or deep? How rhythmic does it feel? Does it feel smooth or coarse? Is it graceful and round, or are there some parts that feel jerky or jagged? Does it feel soothing?

Often we don't breathe out fully, but hurry on to the next inhalation. Take the time to follow the entire length of your exhalation. Stay with it. Patiently wait until it is finished before you take your next breath. It takes some time to release all the used air from the alveoli. There is no need to tighten any muscles to "squeeze" the last air out. Just be patient and let it keep on flowing. Whenever you feel you are trying too hard, release the effort.

Now become aware of the time at the end of the exhalation before the next inhalation begins. There is a brief moment before your lungs call for air. Don't grab for the next breath. Sink into this natural pause and enjoy it. It is a moment of tranquility, as still as a deep, calm pond. The exhalation disappears into it, and then the stillness gives birth to the inhalation. As you observe this stillness, you may find the pause lengthening naturally.

Have a friend read the instructions with plenty of pauses to allow you to explore.

Now attune yourself to what happens at the top of the inhalation, before you feel the need to exhale. There is another pause, another precious moment. It is a full silence that you can relax into. As you let yourself sink into this moment it will expand.

These pauses give rise to a breath in four parts; a releasing exhalation, a still pause, the gift of a new inhalation and a pause. Become absorbed in a meditative way in each part of your breath. No two breaths are the same. Make friends with your breath and get to know each part intimately.

Before you roll over to sit up, take some time to observe the effects this exercise has had on your mind. You have learned a new skill to quieten the mind. You will find you have developed your self-awareness, and practiced being absorbed in the present moment.

Right: Carry this breathing exercise over into the more vigorous asanas.

Chest Opening Exercise—*Awareness of the Breath*

Channeling the breath into movement is centering and helps maintain a steady rhythmic breath.

1 Lie on your back with your knees bent up and your hands palms-down on the floor. To begin, exhale fully.

2 While you inhale, raise your arms up and overhead until the backs of your hands come to rest on or near the floor. Energize your arms so that they extend and lift out of your shoulders to flow through a large arc.

3 Exhale and raise your arms up to bring them back to the starting position. With eyes closed, continue moving between these two movements. Time the movement to follow your breath, not the other way around. Because you keep the flow of air in and out through the nostrils at a steady rate, your arm movements are also constant and graceful.

4 Now become aware of how your torso moves in relation to the arm movements. As you inhale and raise the arms up, feel the natural life of the upper back as it lifts away from the floor. Rest with your arms overhead for several breaths. The upper back will ground more into the floor and your chest will naturally open and promote a lovely full inhalation. Each time your exhale your arms down, tune into the softening down that happens in the torso as it releases into the earth. Moving slowly, with awareness, bring your attention to your pelvis. Can you feel the gentle tilting back and forward with each part of the breath? Take some more time, unhurriedly observing the movements of the body in response to the breath.

Biralasana—*Cat Pose*

This exercise brings awareness and flexibility to the entire length of the spine. The key to awareness is to move slowly. Practice patience and keep an inquiring mind.

1 Begin the pose on all fours with your knees under your hips and your hands just forward of your shoulders.

2 Inhale and concave your back. Move your breastbone forward and up and raise your tailbone up. Keep the back of your neck long as you gaze upward. Pressurize the palms evenly against the floor and avoid slumping into the shoulders.

3 As you exhale, round your back. Your upper back arches naturally in this way, so place particular awareness on the movement of the lower back as it follows this new curve upward as you tuck your pelvis under. Observe how your shoulder blades spread apart and the skin between them stretches. As you finish your exhalation, move your chin toward your breastbone.

4 Repeat 10 more rounds, arching and rounding in time to your breath. Accentuate the curve in the repeats so that it is deeper each time.

EXPLORE

The vertebral column is made up of 33 vertebrae. The bottom nine are fused, but the remaining 24 are not. Narrow your focus to a single vertebra at a time. Mentally go inside to observe its range of movement. Alternatively, begin the movement at the tailbone and concave your back, moving vertebra by vertebra, up the spine, taking as many breaths as you need.

Roll Downs

Working through this sequence will allow you to learn about how undoing, rather than active doing, can deepen a pose.

1 Stand in Tadasana (see page 43) with your feet hip-width apart. You are going to take several breaths to fold forward by rolling down the spine.

2 As you exhale, drop your head forward. Feel how the shoulders want to follow. Release your knees so that they bend slightly. On your next exhalation let the shoulders go and the upper back round more. Your arms hang down vertically, dangling passively out of their sockets. Continue exhaling and rolling down the back in stages, leading with the head. Your knees will bend more the further you roll down. Take as many breaths as you need to release all the way down.

3 Even though your legs are working, your upper body is dangling, hanging out of the hips. Bring a rag-doll quality to the upper body. Move your awareness to the shoulders and relax them fully so that the arms hang loose. Relax the back of the neck so that the crown of the head is the closest part of the head to the floor.

4 Take several rounds of breathing, observing the movements intrinsically related to the breath. As you inhale there is a lifting energy in the core of the body. If your knees are bent enough, a small lengthening occurs from pubic bone to throat. As you exhale your ribs will fall closer to your thighs.

5 When it's time to come up, keep the knees bent and, over several breaths, roll up slowly through the spine, as if you are stacking each vertebra on top of the last. Exhale; release the arms down to the sides.

2a   2b   3

EXPLORE

Repeat the same process, rolling down to each side in turn. Indulge by giving yourself plenty of time.

Sukhasana Forward Fold—*Cross-Legged Forward Fold*

Sukha means content or happy. Spending a few minutes letting yourself soften into this pose is a centering way to start your practice.

1 Begin by sitting in a simple cross-legged position. To work deeper into the hips, slide your heels away from each other so that they rest under the knees. Then take the feet forward so that the shins are in a horizontal line.

2 Become aware of the sitting bones in contact with the floor. This base will act as your anchor as you stretch forward. Place your fingertips on the floor just in front of your legs. Now lengthen the sides of the torso from hips to armpits. Use several breaths to let this releasing take place. When you feel ready, creep the hands away. Work with your breath as you take one or two minutes to slide the hands forward in stages. Only drop your forehead down to the floor if your front ribs come to lie on your legs. Then repeat with the legs crossed the other way.

EXPLORE

Don't become mentally lazy. Stay aware. If you are performing the pose automatically, you might just stay at the point you initially reached. When you use longer holds in a pose, often you will find you can go much deeper and extend yourself to your new edge.

Standing Postures

Within the standing postures you find side bends, backbends, forward bends, twists and balances. With the exception of the inverted positions, they embody the effects of all the other groups of yoga postures.

Regular practice of the standing poses is a great start for all yogis. They increase strength and flexibility in equal parts. Since they extend and integrate the whole body, they help correct imbalances of the vertebral column. They develop grace, endurance, perseverance and concentration. They also help you to feel more energetic and enthusiastic.

Since they involve the whole body, they warm you in preparation for the other poses. Since they are expansive poses, you can more easily see the directions of energy extension as the arms and legs extend out from the spine. You can use these energies to give your poses a lightness. Over time, these poses will even help to bring the spring back into flat feet.

In order to achieve anything in life, we need somewhere to extend from. Standing postures let us develop roots. They allow us to examine how we 'stand on our own two feet' and how to 'stand our ground'. They help us establish a firm base to ensure that the upper body is well supported. In standing poses we play off stability with extension as we practice radiating outward from this steady base.

> *When the body becomes lean, the face glows with delight, the eyes are clear and the body is healthy, one should know success in hatha yoga is approaching.*
>
> HATHA YOGA PRADIPIKA II:78

About Alignment: Your Posture

Your feet need to be well aligned in order to bring good posture to the rest of the body. Stand with your feet a little less than hip-width apart. Feel free to experiment to find the width that gives you the most centered feeling.

From the Ground Up

1 Have a good look at your feet. How are the arches? Do they lift up like little rainbows, or do they collapse downward to produce flat feet or knock-knees? How are your toes? Are they squashed together from years of wearing tight shoes? Are they white with tension as they cling to the ground? Ungrip the toes by lifting them up and spreading them apart. Keeping them stretched away, place them down on the floor.

2 Stand erect once more and feel where the heaviness comes into the feet. Where is the weight centered? Is there more weight placed on the ball of the feet, or the heels? Is one foot taking more weight than another? Rock back and forth to find your center. Keeping the feet on the floor, transfer the weight from left to right and back several times to home in on the center of grounding. Lean in all directions in a large circle. Then slowly reduce the size of the circle until you come to find your centered point.

3 Mentally soften the soles of your feet. Spread the skin. Let your breath come into the feet. They widen and soften with each exhalation. Visualize roots growing downward. By earthing the feet, the rest of the body is free to expand and lengthen up to the sky.

Avoid standing poses in acute cases of asthma, colitis, nervous disorders or cardiac problems. Don't jump in or out of the poses if you are pregnant, menstruating or if you have back or knee injuries.

From the Pelvis Up

1 Anterior tilt. Stand with your hands on your hips, fingers pointing forward, so that your index fingers rest on top of the hipbones and press into the waist. Pelvis means basin in Latin. Tilt your pelvis forward, just as if it were a basin and you were tipping water out of the front of it. Your fingers will point down and your thumbs will lift up. Feel how the curve in your lower back accentuates and your chest lifts a bit. This action makes the knees push back too.

Further steps overleaf

1

EXPLORE

Sit on the floor and give your feet a little massage first. Do small karate chops on the soles of the feet. Make loose fists and do some light pounding. Rub your hands briskly over the feet using the friction to build warmth. Now you might find it easier to become aware of how your feet contact the earth.

2

2 Posterior tilt. Now tilt the pelvis the other way, as if you were pouring out water from the back. Your fingers will rise up and your thumbs move down. Observe how this changes your posture. Your lower back curve will flatten and the fronts of your knees will move forward. The chest tends to slump, abdominal length shortens and shoulders roll forward. Feel how this affects your neck too. If you are not sure, exaggerating the movements might help make the dynamic clearer.

3 Come back to the center, so your pelvis is not tipped forward or back, but centered. Take time to feel how it is, mentally comparing it to your normal way of standing.

By taking time to move in between the anterior and posterior pelvic tilt positions, you will become familiar with the trickle-on effects of them both on the rest of your body. A truly centered pelvis would actually be too unstable to carry us well, so people tend to have a pelvis tilted either one way or the other. Ideally this position would be just off center, rather than strongly so. Still standing, find a more centered position for your pelvis. Take time to scan through your body, observing how it feels when comparing it to your normal way of carrying yourself. Slowly move around the room like this, exploring some new possibilities for your carriage and movement.

Elongating the Curves of the Spine

1 Stand with your back to a corner wall, or on the edge of a doorframe. Take your feet about 1ft (30cm) away from the wall, and a little bit apart, with the outside edges of the feet parallel. Lean against the wall so that your body contacts the wall at the sacrum and the thoracic curve. The small of the back (lumbar region) will arch away from the wall. How easily the back of your head comes to the wall depends on the curves of your spine. If your upper back is very flat, your throat will feel constricted. If your upper back is very rounded, it will be more difficult to bring your head comfortably to the wall. If your chin juts out and the back of the neck shortens, find a midway position for the head. Gently bring your floating ribs down, so they don't jut out. Don't bend your knees. Bring the tops of the thighs back slightly so that the front of the groin opens.

2 The spine is most effectively lengthened by undoing, rather than doing. Take plenty of time to release so that the spine can elongate upward. If you actively work the muscles that run along the spine then they will contract and actually shorten the vertebral column. Likewise, there is no need to raise the shoulders up to grow taller. Instead, let go with each exhalation. Let your tailbone be heavy so it eases down toward the floor. Keep your weight well grounded through your feet. As you continue to lengthen, feel the very small movements that ripple along the spine in connection with the breath. Are there any areas of your spine that feel blocked? Concentrate on softening the tight spots. When you move away from the wall, walk softly around the room feeling the effects of this exercise.

EXPLORE

Stay in your habitual standing position for long enough without moving until the sensations begin to intensify. Then take this feedback and see what you need to do to realign and prevent the discomfort coming to those points. Do this when you are sitting in your habitual way on your favorite armchair too.

Tadasana—*Mountain Pose*

This pose connects you to both earth and sky. It is a wonderful exercise in centering and being able to respond to situations from a solid base. Begin and end each of the standing poses with this centered position. Use it as a chance to hear your body's feedback to what happened in the last pose. Although you appear steady as a mountain, you are not as hard as a rock in this pose. Externally your mountain is still, but bring it alive from the inside, where it feels dynamic and alive, responding to every breath. Practice Tadasana whenever possible throughout the day.

1 Stand with your feet a little less than hip-width apart, with the outside edges of your feet parallel. Follow the instructions for softening the feet on page 41. While your feet ground downward, move your awareness to your legs and get a sense of extending up toward the sky starting at the ankle joints. Let your pelvis be in a neutral position (see previous page). The spine, supported by the pelvis, is freed to lengthen upward. It is perfectly possible to stand erect and be relaxed at the same time. Exhale tension out of the spine so it is released to grow taller. Get a sense of your arms dangling from the shoulder sockets. Let them just hang, and completely let go. As your shoulders soften down, the neck and head float and rise up out of them. Release the mouth, tongue and jaw, observing as you do so whether this allows other more distant parts of the body to release too. Bring a sense of weightlessness to the head. Visualize it as a helium-filled balloon on the end of a stick, your spine. Mentally sweep over your body to see where the heaviness is.

2 Check in with your breathing. Release the diaphragm muscle. Take slow, deep, steady breaths. Feel the ripple-like effect of each breath on the spine. Quite different from an upward movement induced by muscle tension, feel the lifting energy with each inhalation. Your body has its own innate intelligence. Be curious! Follow your breath to feel where it lets your body open and expand. Explore any subtle effects that your exhalation has on it.

Virabhadrasana II—*Warrior II*

As if you were aiming a bow and arrow at your target, maintain a perfect mental focus over your middle finger during this pose. Strong legs give self-reliance and independence and the raised head, fearlessness.

1 From Tadasana take the feet wide apart, so that when your arms are stretched out, your ankles will be underneath them. Rotating from the top of the thigh, turn the right leg and foot inward 15 degrees. Turn the left leg and foot out 90 degrees. This tends to alter the position of the hips. Bring your hands onto your hips to help you compare them. If your right hip is higher and more forward than the left hip, adjust so that they are in line.

2 Bend your left knee to a 90-degree angle, not more. If your knee is positioned in front of your ankle, then you need to widen your stance. As the toes of your left foot are facing out to the side, your knee should be obscuring your view of all except your big toe. Look down the front of your torso to check that the ribs on both sides are even.

3 Rotate your upper arms outward so that the palms turn out. Then raise your arms until they are parallel with the floor. Finally, rotate just the forearms so that the palms face down to the floor—the creases of your elbows will remain facing upward. Drop your shoulders down. Become aware of two lines of energy radiating from your spine out to your fingertips. Use this feeling to help keep your arms parallel to the floor. Turn your head to gaze at your left index finger. Take 10 slow, steady breaths before repeating on the right side.

EXPLORE

To protect your knees, they must be facing the same direction as the toes of their respective feet.

Parsvakonasana—*Side Angle Stretch*

From the steady base of the legs, now reach out with energy to stretch fully the entire side of the body.

1 From Tadasana bring the legs into the same position as Virabhadrasana II (see previous page). More weight tends to come onto the front leg, so during the pose press into the floor with your back foot to spread your weight evenly between both feet. Stretch your left arm up and out to the side. The right side of the torso will naturally lengthen, so pay particular attention to extending out of your left hip to lengthen the underside of the torso as well.

2 Bring your left elbow to your thigh. Use the elbow to press the knee back so your left inner thigh will lengthen. The kneecap should point in the same direction as your middle toe, not in the direction of your big toe. This elbow pressure aids the twist in the torso so your torso can rotate upward. Stretch your right arm straight up, reaching with your fingers as high as you can. Take a few breaths before proceeding to the full asana. If this is where you stay for today, hold this position for five to ten breaths.

3 For the full pose, bring your left hand to cup the floor near your little toe. With your right arm overhead, turn the palm to the direction you are bending and bring the arm to form a straight line from right foot to right hand. You may need to widen your stance or bend the left knee more to lower your hips. Gaze up to the sky from under your upper arm. Build the time in the pose to 10 breaths. Repeat on the other side.

EXPLORE

If the head feels uncomfortable looking up in the standing poses, look straight ahead. If you find balance difficult, then gaze down to the floor.

Utkatasana—*Mighty Pose*

Don't let your breath harden or become irregular as you hold this strong pose, which strengthens willpower and determination.

1 Stand in Tadasana with your big toes and inner heels together. Keeping the heels anchored, deeply bend the knees. Reach out your arms in front of you to press your palms together. Inhale your arms up overhead. If possible, make your elbows straight as you do this. Lift everything up from the hips except the shoulders. Unhunch your shoulders and keep as much distance as you can between your earlobes and upper arms.

2 Gaze upward. Press the pubic bone forward and upward to flatten out the lower back. Draw your abdominal muscles in and up to support this flattening. Work the muscles along the spine strongly to bring it more vertical. Bend the knees to take your hips lower and press the inner thighs together. Stay for five breaths.

EXPLORE

For more of a challenge, take your thighbones parallel to the floor for five breaths. The trunk will naturally want to lean forward. To deepen the pose, lift the abdomen away from the legs to resist this lean and bring the back more perpendicular to the floor.

Virabhadrasana I—*Warrior I*

This all-involving pose works the arms and legs, strengthens the back and opens the chest.

1 Stand with your legs about 4ft (1.2m) apart. Turn your whole right leg and foot deeply inward 60 degrees. Turn your left leg and foot out 90 degrees and swivel your whole upper body so it faces over your left leg. Open the groin by letting your left hip move forward to align with the right. If this is difficult, turn the back leg and foot in deeper. An easier alternative is to have the feet parallel and lift the back heel up a little off the floor (see below).

2 Bend your left knee to a 90-degree angle. Keep your back leg straight by pressing the back heel away to open the back of the knee.

3 Take your arms out to the sides, turn the palms up and raise the arms overhead to join the palms. Gaze at your thumbs. Stretch up from the hips to the fingertips. As you breathe deeply, feel the stretch of skin on the chest and abdomen. Stay for 10 breaths, and maintain perfect awareness as you come out of the pose and move to the right side.

A

Alternative ʌ **Heel lifted.**

An easier alternative for beginners is to have the feet parallel and lift the back heel off the floor. If you have trouble balancing, step the front foot a little to the side. Sometimes people unconsciously hunch their shoulders when attempting to press their palms

together. Until your shoulder flexibility develops, take your palms apart and arms parallel and check if this releases it. If you still feel "bad" shoulder tension, then lower your arms 10 or 20 degrees forward, with attention to spreading the shoulder blades well apart.

EXPLORE

In these wide stance poses, have your feet lined up so the heel of the front foot bisects the center of the back foot. You can even draw a line up the center of your mat.

Trikonasana—*Triangle Pose*

This pose has five rays of energy: two arms stretching away, two legs stretching out and down and a fifth line running from the tailbone as it extends toward the crown of the head.

1 From Tadasana, jump or step the feet 4–4½ft (1.2–1.4m) apart. Turning from the thighs, rotate the right foot inward 15 degrees and turn the left foot out 90 degrees. Level off your hips. If your legs are not working fully, your kneecaps will slump down and inward, so activate your thigh muscles to ensure the kneecaps track over the toes. Take your left hand near your knee. Trikonasana is a strong side stretch so the body needs to be on one plane. Your hipbones, shoulders and hands should be along the same line as your feet. To open the chest and keep your single-plane alignment, wrap the other arm around the back to wedge the hand by the inner thigh, or else take hold of the back of your trousers. Assist this action by bending the front knee.

2 Draw your left sitting bone down toward your right inner heel so your hips move to the right. As you do this, straighten your left leg and slide the left hand down the leg or possibly to the floor as pictured. If you find your shoulders have come forward of your feet, and your buttocks have moved back, adjust your alignment by bringing your left hand higher up your leg. Roll your right shoulder back and enjoy the openness in the chest for several breaths before eventually releasing your right arm to vertical. Stretch out well from abdomen to feet, and from shoulders toward each hand. Intensify the line of energy from tailbone to crown of the head by sliding the shoulder blades away from the ears to keep the back of the neck long. Tuck the chin slightly in, turn the head and gaze at the right thumb. Stay for five to ten breaths, then repeat on the right side.

EXPLORE

Sit on the floor with your legs in front of you. When your thighs are relaxed, you will be able to move your kneecap from side to side. Activate your thigh muscles to straighten the legs and raise your heels off the ground. Now you won't be able to move the kneecap from side to side. Use this activation of the thighs, not forced or locked, but firm and aware, in Trikonasana.

Prasarita Padottanasana—*Wide Leg Stretch*

In asanas the arms and legs often act as levers to work the spine. But make sure they work with the rest of your body and breath, not forcefully overriding them.

1 From Tadasana, step your feet wide apart. Have your toes facing straight ahead and the outside edges of the feet parallel. Bring your hands to your hips. With the heels heavy on the floor, let the tailbone drop down to the earth. This helps make space between the vertebrae of the lower back and protects them from compressing. Firm the front of the thigh muscles, open the groin and expand the breastbone up to the sky as you look up and back. Hold for several breaths.

2 On an exhalation, fold forward. If possible, position both palms on the floor, shoulder-width apart. Have your upper arms parallel. If you are still developing your hamstring flexibility, bend your knees if necessary to bring your fingertips to the floor. Unhunch the shoulders by sliding the shoulder blades up toward the hips. Walk the hands back as they lever you deeper into a forward bend. When it is time to come up, bring your hands back onto your hips. Firm the thigh and abdominal muscles and inhale to come up.

EXPLORE

Interlace your fingers behind your back and take your arms overhead. Firm your front thigh muscles as your thumbs move toward the floor.

Uttanasana—*Intense Forward Stretch*

If you suffer from hypertension, keep the trunk parallel to the floor and place your hands on a chair or table. Begin working through this sequence with Roll Downs (see page 38)

Using a Wall

1 To maintain length in the front of the torso, practice using the wall. Stand with your feet apart and about 1ft (30cm) away from the wall. Lean your buttocks to the wall so your sitting bones touch it. Hold your elbows and take the arms overhead. Bend the knees and extend the torso up so the top of the breastbone moves away from the pubic bone. With knees strongly bent, reach your torso forward. Stretch as far out with the elbows as possible. Finally fold over your legs and let your upper body hang for 10 breaths or more. With each inhalation the torso can lengthen more, and with each exhalation the crease at the top of the thighs can deepen. If you can't work into this position in a relaxed fashion, bend the knees more or walk the feet further away from the wall. Come up on an inhalation.

1

2 Move away from the wall. Bring your hands on your hips, inhale, lift your breastbone and look up. Exhale, hinge at the hips to reach forward so the crown of the head moves in as big an arc as possible. Imagine your hip sockets and pelvis rolling forward over your thighbones, which stay vertical.

2

3 With your knees bent or straight, grasp your legs or ankles, or loop your big toes with finger and thumb. Increase the stretch by flattening out the back and stretching your sternum forward. Angle your sitting bones toward the sky, lengthen the back of your waist. Tilt your pelvis forward as if aiming to press your navel to your thighs—you will feel the stretch in the back of your thighs intensify.

3

4 Then exhale and fold forward to hold the pose. If your knees are bent, use each exhalation to work the legs straighter. If your legs are straight, firm the front thigh muscles and bring your hips forward to bring the hip joints directly over your ankles.

Check that your face is relaxed. Free the upper lip so your cheeks feel like they are dropping down toward the floor. If you have forgotten to breathe, check whether the pose is too strong for you and ease back until you free the breath.

4

EXPLORE

Working the feet correctly in the standing poses helps retrain flat feet over time. If you have flat feet, lift your toes up to work the arches in the standing postures. Alternatively, anchor the inner heel and mound of the big toe and, without rolling the ankles out, lift your arches like rainbows.

Parsvottanasana—*Chest to Leg Extension*

With the prayer position behind your back, bow to your inner light in this strong forward bend.

1 From Tadasana, take your feet 3–4ft (1–1.2m) apart. Turn your left knee and foot deeply inward to 60 degrees, and your right leg and foot out 90 degrees. Your left hip will be further back than your right hip. Bring it forward so both hips are level and you can better line up your breastbone with the inside of your right thigh.

2 To form prayer position, bring your backs of your hands to your back. Walk your fingers up between the shoulder blades, then roll your shoulders and elbows back as you press the mounds of your thumbs together. An alternative for tighter shoulders is to interlace your hands so knuckles rest on either side of your spine, or else to grasp your elbows behind your back. As a preparation for folding forward, inhale, lift your chest and look up.

3 Think forward and out before thinking of the downward movement over your right thigh. Exhale as you reach out of the hips to sweep up, out, forward and then down. It is easy to unknowingly bend the knees in this pose so keep the thigh muscles activated and press down through the back heel. Stay for five to ten breaths before repeating on the second side.

2

3

A

Alternative A

While you develop your flexibility in this pose, practicing using a chair keeps your back straight and your chest open to encourage full breathing.

EXPLORE

To help your balance, mentally anchor down your front big toe and the heel of your back foot. If you still feel unsteady, step the back foot out to the side.

Pavritta Trikonasana—*Revolved Triangle Pose*

This advanced pose combines balance, twisting and forward bending. In the wide stance poses, the further apart the feet are, the greater the spinal extension, but the more difficult it becomes to balance.

1 Stand with your feet 3–4ft (1–1.2m) apart. Turn your left foot and leg well inward to about 60 degrees and turn the right foot out 90 degrees. Bring your left hip forward so that it's level with the right hip. Stretch your left arm up in the air and take several breaths, getting a sense of the full extension all the way from the left ankle to the left hand.

2 On an exhalation, reach the left arm and torso forward and down to bring the left hand to cup the floor by the right little toe. If the hand doesn't reach, place the hand on the seat of a chair or on a stack of books. With both feet and the left hand anchored, stretch the right hip back to help the extension of the spine out of the hips. Rotate the torso well to the right so the navel and heart open up to the sky. Take the right arm straight up into the air and gaze up at your right thumb.

1

2

EXPLORE

Looking down to the floor makes it easier to balance while you increase the twist in the trunk. Take several breaths gazing at the floor to allow a deeper rotation. Finally turn the head to look forward and slowly up to the top thumb.

Forward Bends

Sometimes in our outward-looking lives, we ignore messages from inside. Folding into ourselves quietens the mind and encourages a meditative mindset. Forward bends foster the ability to listen to our intuitive self, to our heart.

Gravity often helps us fold forward; we can go deeper into the pose by yielding rather than forcing. From the seated position, we don't even have to be concerned with balancing, and can take energy and support from the earth. The forward bends are a little like the fetal position and have nurturing qualities for when we need to feel protected.

As you fold in half from your hips, your head comes closer to your feet. The two extremes of the body come together and help you find your center. Life is full of dualities. Rather than operating from one end of the spectrum, you can find a better balance; moderation and the middle path in our world view and way of living.

By increasing pressure on the organs of the abdomen, forward bends are particularly beneficial to the digestive system. As the pelvis houses nerve ganglions of the parasympathetic nervous system, they also help balance the nervous systems. The parasympathetic nervous system directs our "rest and restore" response. Forward bends are therefore helpful for those with active, busy (sympathetic nervous system-dominant) lives, and for anyone who seeks healing and better all-round health.

Forward bends can be done in a very active way, with strong breathing to help release deeper into the postures. Alternatively, when you are experiencing menstrual discomfort, feel fatigued or need to revive, they can be done softly, and made more restorative using a chair or a bolster. Rest the forehead on a chair seat covered by a soft blanket. If you are more flexible, use a bolster (For an example see page 112).

Don't overdo the forward bends if you suffer from severe depression. Focus on backbends instead. Those suffering hypertension do best to keep their head above their heart.

Forward bends maintain integrity of the spine, but proceed cautiously if you have back pain. If a weakness exists or if you are recovering from an injury, it is always best to build your practice in a slow and steady way. If you suffer from disc problems, that section of the spine needs to be kept concave and should not be bent forward until it is ready.

Work with a teacher to implement forward bends into your practice bit by bit as your back strengthens. Allow 24 hours after the practice for your body to give you its feedback.

Below: Develop patience and the ability to stay longer in the forward bends.

About Alignment—*Discovering the Action of the Pelvis and Hips*

It's worthwhile investing some time experimenting to discover how to get the most benefit out of forward bends.

1 Sit erect in your chair and place your hands on your waist. Lower your chin to your chest, then bring your head down toward your thighs. You will feel the stretch mostly along the sides of the spine. Observe how your shoulders hunch and your back rounds. You might also notice that it's difficult to take deep breaths.

2 Now sit up straight once again and lower your hands from your waist to your hips. Inhale, expand the chest, lengthen your spine up and gaze forward. As you exhale, fold forward, leading with the chest. With this movement you hinge from the hips. Compared with the last exercise, the spine is kept relatively straight (which protects the intervertebral discs) and you will feel the stretch more in the hips and back thighs than in the spine. This is the movement required by the yoga forward bends. Practice these two variations a couple more times so you are clear in your mind about the difference. Imprint the memory of this second exercise in your body so you can bring it alive during every yoga forward bend you will encounter in the future.

2

3

3 It helps if we understand where we place our seat when sitting erect. The two sitting bones (ischial tuberosities) act as little anchors to the earth. As you sit on the floor, reach under your buttocks and move your buttock flesh away, in a direction 45 degrees back and out to the side, to help your sitting bones to make contact with the ground.

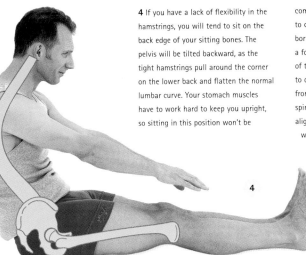

4 If you have a lack of flexibility in the hamstrings, you will tend to sit on the back edge of your sitting bones. The pelvis will be tilted backward, as the tight hamstrings pull around the corner on the lower back and flatten the normal lumbar curve. Your stomach muscles have to work hard to keep you upright, so sitting in this position won't be comfortable. It also creates a tendency to concave the chest. A forward bend born from this position will inevitably be a forward bend from the waist, instead of the hips. Apart from closing the chest to deep breathing, by pressuring the fronts of the intervertebral discs, the spine will not maintain a healthy alignment. The ideal starting position will be sitting right on the center of the sitting bones so that as you fold your body forward, you will roll forward to perch more on the front edge of your sitting bones.

5 While sitting on the floor, touch your lower back. If your lower back still flattens or rounds out instead of keeping its usual inward curve, then your pelvis will be tilting backward. As you need to move from sitting on the back edge of the sitting bones to being on their center, modify your starting position. Lift your seat with folded blankets, and/or bend your knees. Use one or both of these adjustments in your forward bends for as many months as it takes for your body to loosen.

6 It is better to do a smaller-looking forward bend with correct alignment than a seemingly deeper forward bend, which at worst may be injurious and at best doesn't really help release the areas that are chronically tight. Keep the length in the spine by extending the tailbone and crown of the head away from each other. As you fold forward, stretch your tailbone back and away from the crown of the head. Moving the sitting bones back increases the stretch in the hamstrings.

7 As you fold forward, visualize your thighbones staying still. It is actually the sockets of the hip joints that can rotate around the heads of the thighbones to tilt the pelvis forward. When you can achieve this, the concavity in the lumbar spine will remain for the first part of the forward bend. Test this by placing your hand on your lower back to feel if you have the same curve during the first part of the forward bend. Toward the end of your stretch forward, you will feel the lumbar spine begin to curve outward.

8 Let go of your desire to reach your forehead to your knees. Instead, first aim the navel to the thighs. As you hinge more at the hips, your chest will come closer to your knees, and only after this will the nose come toward the shins.

Dandasana—*Staff Pose*

Dandasana is the base from which we fold forward into many forward bends.

Sit with your legs straight out in front. If it is hard to sit with the back erect in this pose, and you tip back, sit on one or two folded blankets. Place your fingertips or palms on the floor by the buttocks. Roll the thighbones inward so that the inner thighs come together. Have the fronts of the kneecaps and the toes pointing straight upward.

Straighten the knees so the backs of the knees are stretched. Let the arms lengthen. Let the breastbone float up, but not at the cost of shortening the back. Ensure your chin is not jutting out, but is kept parallel to the floor. Imagine your head floating on the top of your spine like a helium balloon on the top of a stick. Lighten your thoughts!

EXPLORE

Because this position is outwardly simpler than many others, it provides a good opportunity to take your attention inward. Take slow, conscious breaths. In this position it is possible to focus not only on the forward and sideward expansion of the torso, but also on the expansion of the back of the torso as you inhale and the lungs fill with air.

Virasana—*Hero Pose*

Although children sit like this quite naturally, older, stiffer bodies can find this pose uncomfortable. Use props as necessary while you regain your flexibility.

2

3

1 Kneel on the floor with your knees together and feet wide apart. As you sit down between your feet, use your fingers to "iron" your calf muscles out to the sides and down toward the heels.

2 Place your hands on the soles of your upturned feet. Lift up from your pubic bone to the notch of the throat. Lift up on the back of the body too, from the tailbone to the crown of the head.

3 If your buttocks don't come down to the floor, then create as much height as you need to be comfortable but still with a

degree of challenge. Use bolsters, cushions or folded blankets as a prop, or an old telephone book; each time you practice, tear out a few pages or fold the blanket less thickly so that over time you are able to sit comfortably on the floor.

4 If you experience knee pain, place a canvas belt or thin folded scarf deeply in the crease of the knees as they bend.

5 If this position gives pain on the tops of the feet, place some cushioning underneath the fronts of the ankles.

EXPLORE

Forward bend from this pose. Lean forward onto your hands, or, if you are more flexible, stretch the arms all the way forward with fingers interlaced.

Trianga Mukhaikapada Paschimottanasana—
Three Limbed Forward Bend

If forward-bending Virasana is too much of a challenge for now, warm yourself up by practicing one leg at a time.

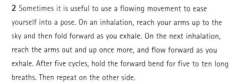

1 From Dandasana, bend your right leg back to bring the foot to the floor next to the buttocks. As in Virasana, "iron" your calf flesh out to the right. As you will tend to tilt to the left, mentally let your right sitting bone be heavy so that you stay balanced.

2

2 Sometimes it is useful to use a flowing movement to ease yourself into a pose. On an inhalation, reach your arms up to the sky and then fold forward as you exhale. On the next inhalation, reach the arms out and up once more, and flow forward as you exhale. After five cycles, hold the forward bend for five to ten long breaths. Then repeat on the other side.

Alternative A
To align the spine and better balance the hips, place a support under one buttock.

A

EXPLORE

Try this way of working in some poses. If you will hold a pose for 15 breaths, use the first five to adjust and deepen the posture. For the remaining 10 breaths, remain steady at a still point. At this point you still the fluctuations of the body, and are moving neither from nor toward any point. Be receptive to your observations.

Janu Sirsasana—*Head Beyond The Knee Pose*

As this pose stretches out the lower back, it is wonderful after backbends and inversions.

3

1 From Dandasana, bend your right leg out to the side so the sole of the foot comes close to, but not actually touching, the left inner thigh. Keep your left leg straight by opening the back of the knee to the floor.

2 Stretch your left heel away so the knee and toes point straight up. Tilt the pelvis forward so you are sitting on the front side of the sitting bones. Before you think about going forward, it's useful to sit erect and breathe yourself taller for a short while. When you are ready, inhale your arms overhead.

3 Exhale as you extend forward to grasp your calf, ankle or foot. Inhale, lift your chest and look up. Exhale, bend your elbows to the side, and fold forward maintaining a flat back and open chest. Hold five to ten breaths before repeating the other side.

Alternative A

To help establish a forward pelvic tilt, sit on a folded blanket. If you find that you round your back in this pose, loop a belt around your foot and focus on lengthening the trunk.

A

EXPLORE

Keep the knee and toes of the straight leg pointing upward, ankle flexed and heel stretched away in all the straight leg forward bends.

Ardha Baddha Padma Paschimottanasana—
Bound Half Lotus Forward Fold

Due to the position of the arms in this hip-opening stretch, it is difficult to "cheat" by rounding the shoulders. Warming up the hip will help prevent knee problems and assist the movement of the knee toward the earth. Apart from this warm up, you can practice the ankle to knee pose (see page 68).

1 Warm up the hip by cradling your right leg. If cradling is difficult, then hold the knee and foot in both hands and push them slightly together. Slowly move the leg back and forth as you would rock a baby. Keep your right foot flexed as you slowly move the knee beyond the armpit. If you find this movement easy, then lift the right foot up higher.

2 Take the bent leg to the floor and out to the side. Hold the top of the foot, and slide it onto the other thigh until the ankle is resting on the thigh—if you only bring the top of the foot to the thigh, the ligaments of the outside of the foot risk being overstretched. Reach around with your right hand and take hold of the foot.

Alternative A

If you can't reach your foot, loop a belt around your shin and hold both ends with your left hand.

3 Stretch forward and take your right hand to the right foot, ankle or shin. Release your left knee down to the floor. Hold for five to ten breaths. Repeat on the other side.

EXPLORE

Remind yourself that it is irrelevant how far you look like you go in a pose. The important thing is to reach the point where you can learn and change. Measure your posture not by how flexible you are, but by how steady your breath is.

Paschimottanasana—*Stretch on the West Side of the Body*

Traditionally yoga asana practice is done facing north or east. In this pose, as you fold toward the east, you stretch the side of the body facing west.

1 Sit tall in Dandasana and wriggle forward so you come onto the front edge of your sitting bones. If your hamstrings are tight and you feel your torso leaning backward, instead of being vertical, then sit on folded blankets and/or bend your knees up a little.

2 To avoid the undesirable habit of rounding the back, first experiment with the position of your arms. Bring your hands into the prayer pose behind the back (as in Parsvottanasana on page 52). If you find this too difficult, cup both elbows behind your back.

3 On an exhalation, fold forward, tilting the pelvis forward and using your abdominal muscles. The position of the arms means your chest is kept open.

4 Stay and breathe. You should feel your palms spread apart as the back of the trunk expands with each inhalation. If you can't access this movement, ease off on the intensity until you are able to free up the back for the breath. Imprint this feeling of the straight back and open chest on your body's memory, so that you can repeat it during the next stage.

5 Now practice the classic Paschimottanasana. Sit in Dandasana. Keep your knees and toes pointing to the sky. Lengthen from the tailbone to the crown of the head. After several breaths "growing" the spine, inhale and raise the arms overhead, then exhale the arms and torso forward. Remember the feeling from the first exercise—keep the chest open and the breath free. Depending on your flexibility, hold one wrist around the feet, hook your toes, grasp the sides of your feet or ankles or loop a belt around the balls of the feet. Take long, slow breaths for 10 to 15 rounds.

EXPLORE

Experiment with different arm positions. Try bending forward with the arms in the Gomukhasana position (see page 68), interlacing your fingers at the back of the neck, or with your fingers interlaced behind your back and arms lifting up.

Upavista Konasana—*Seated Wide Angle Pose Sequence*

Have patience as you hold this pose. Wait for the body to let you in.

1 Sit with your legs out to the sides at about a 90-degree angle. In this pose it is easy to let the kneecaps roll backward or forward so check that your kneecaps and toes point straight up. Place your right hand, palm up, on your right thigh. Inhale and raise your left arm up, then curve over to the right so the sides of your body curve out like a rainbow. Keep your left shoulder on the same plane as your right, not in front of it. "Puff" out the left side ribs and draw the right side ribs into the body. Imagine the spaces between the left sides of each vertebra stretching apart. Slide your right hand down your leg. Hold for at least five breaths.

2 Now twist your torso toward the floor as you lower your left shoulder and arm. Bring the left hand near the right to stretch over your right leg. Turn the toes back and extend through both heels. Anchor down through the left sitting bone. Hold the pose for five to ten breaths.

3 Now you have arrived at Upavista Konasana. Walk the hands in a wide arc toward the center. Ease back a little so you can tune into the sensation of the trunk lifting out of the hips. Slide the hands forward as you release in stages over about a minute.

4 When you have completed this sequence on both sides of the body, support under your knees with your hands as you bring your legs together for Dandasana.

CAUTION

You should not experience inner knee pain in this pose. If you do, make sure you are working the legs by stretching out through the heels, and firming the thigh muscles to the bone. Narrow the distance between the legs and ease off on the stretch.

Baddha Konasana—*Cobbler's Pose*

Translated from Sanskrit as Bound Angle Pose, this position is also called Cobbler's Pose because it is the position in which shoemakers in India sit to work.

1 Raise your seat with a support like a cushion and bring the soles of your feet together. Draw your heels up close toward you. Use the pressure of your hands on the floor behind you to tilt the pelvis forward. As you do so, let the breastbone float up. These two movements will begin the opening along the inner thighs and groin. With the support of your hands behind you, move the knees away from each other, back and down to the floor. If your hips are tight, this may be as far as you go in this pose for today.

2 If your pelvis tips forward easily, you can dispense with the cushion before bending your elbows into the calves and binding the feet with your hands. Inhale and create the sensation of the torso lifting out of the pelvis. Exhale and deepen the fold. On each inhalation, lengthen right up from pubic bone to throat; each exhalation is an opportunity to move out and down. Rather than butterflying the knees up and down, work with the breath to soften the tight areas. Breathe evenly and repeat for five to ten rounds.

EXPLORE

Sit on the floor in this position whenever possible. Lean back against the sofa in Cobbler's Pose while you watch television.

Supta Padangustasana—*Reclining Big Toe Pose*

This pose keeps the back stable and helps prevent it from overstretching by moving the stretch more into the hamstrings. For those who are recovering from a herniated disc, this pose is a safe forward bend to practice on the road to recovery.

1 Lie on your back with your knees bent up. Lift your right leg up and loop a belt around the ball of the foot. Straighten the leg. As you inhale, imagine a line of energy from right buttock to right heel. As you exhale, yield to stretch the back of the leg more.

2 Release tension in the shoulders. Check that the chin is not jutting up in the air—if it is, slide the back of the head away to lengthen the neck and bring it down.

3 If you are ready to move onto stage two, straighten the left leg along the floor and stretch out through both heels. As your flexibility grows, your leg will form an acute angle with your torso. Then you will be able to work the pose by holding the big toe of the raised foot. Until this comes, use the belt.

1

After one to two minutes in this position, inhale and curl your head and upper back off the floor to bring your nose to your knee. Walk your hands higher up the belt. Hold for seven breaths and when you exhale down, keep the hands at that height and your body may be able to accept the increased stretch.

3

4 For this next stage, it is important to keep the left leg straight as it acts as your anchor. In the beginning, use your left hand to press down on the top of your left thigh. Holding the belt or side of your foot, take your right leg out to the side. Although you may not get that high this practice, aim to take your toes to the floor at shoulder level. Do this movement slowly so you don't lose the grounding force of the left upper thigh and left heel. If you start to tip, come back up and press both sides of the sacrum down to the floor before lowering down again. Hold for five to ten breaths.

5 Come back to center and hold your big toe, or both ends of the belt, in your left hand. Turn your toes inward and anchor down the sacrum on the right side. It helps to press down with your thumb at the root of the thigh. Take the leg over to the left and hold for five to ten breaths. Come back to stretching through the center before lowering the leg down to repeat on the second side.

EXPLORE

Before you do this hip-releasing sequence, lie flat and look at your feet. Your toes will be turned out—measure how much the toes of each foot are turned out, checking the difference between sides. This sequence releases the hips. Visually measure it again after each side.

Gomukhasana—*Cow Face Pose*

Sometimes the poses we find most difficult are the very ones we can benefit most

from practicing regularly.

1 Warm the hips up first by sitting cross-legged. Take the left ankle and place it on the top of the right knee. Make sure it is the ankle, not the outer part of the top of the foot so that the ligaments in that area are not stretched too much. If your top shin is more or less parallel to the floor, then you can place your hands on the floor in front and stretch forward. Otherwise, breathe into the hips from an upright position to help loosen them. Repeat on the other side. Another useful warm-up is cradling the leg (see page 62).

2 Kneel, then cross your left knee over your right knee. As you sit back in the space between your feet, let your right knee stay on the floor. Your left knee will lift and ideally sit neatly on top of the right. However, if you are less flexible it may come up in mid-air. Raise your seat a little with folded blankets if you would like to make the pose easier.

3 Take your right arm straight up in the air. Rotating from the shoulder, turn the little finger to the front. Extend the distance from right hip to fingertips. Then bend the elbow to lower your forearm behind you. Hold the elbow with your left hand and take several breaths as you ease your right hand further down your back. When your right shoulder has grown accustomed to the stretch, release your left arm down. From the left shoulder, rotate the arm so your thumb turns inward then back. Bend the arm to grasp your hands together. Move the back of the head back—don't let the head tilt down to one side. As you sit tall and breathe 10 to 15 breaths, be aware of the expansion of the right side ribs in this position. Repeat on the second side.

Alternative A

For tight shoulders, grasp a soft belt and use time and the breath to help you inch your hands together.

EXPLORE

If this pose comes easily to you, lower the arms and lean forward onto the hands. Then try bringing your heels forward so they are on the same transverse plane as your buttocks. Now place your hands on the floor in front of you and lean forward to deepen the stretch.

After Forward Folding

These stretches act as counter poses after some intense forward bending.

Purvottanasana—*Stretch on the East Side of the Body*
From Dandasana, lean back, point the toes, lift your hips high
and fully expand your chest.

Purvottanasana—*Easier Version*
Begin with bent knees, lift the hips and chest up,
then stretch the chin away.

Z Pose
Kneel on a cushioned surface if you like. Stretch the arms
forward, parallel to the floor. Tuck the tailbone under,
open the groin and lean back to form a "Z" shape.

Savasana Variation—*Corpse Pose Variation*
Resting in Corpse Pose with the arms overhead brings
a slight backbend to balance the body.

Backbends

Like the forward bends, the backbends help

keep the spine supple and well aligned to

promote good functioning of the nerves

that innervate the rest of the body.

Backbends

Sit erect, take a deep inhalation, look up and notice how the spine seems to lengthen, grow and extend. Congratulations! You have begun a lovely backbend!

If you think of what you do everyday, you will notice many of your activities involve bending forward. Sitting at a desk to work, at a table to eat, or when driving, even doing housework or gardening, all tend to shorten the front of the body. The common habit of looking at the ground while walking can also put a stoop into otherwise good posture. Backbends realign the spine, counteract rounded shoulders and help us move with poise and grace.

Backbends are exciting, energy raising and warming. Repeat any active backbend a few times in a cold room and you will soon feel the heat created. Backbends keep the spine young and supple. They activate the abdominal region and stimulate blood supply to the kidneys, reproductive system and digestive organs.

The vertebral column houses the main subtle energy pathway, the Sushumna Nadi. Backbends help shunt energy up the spine and through the chakras, the centers of energy, along the way. Working especially from the second to fifth chakras, energy blockages are released and stagnant areas invigorated in this way.

You need courage, determination and will-power to hold strong backbends, the very same qualities that are linked to the third chakra at the solar plexus. Backbends build character, strength and confidence, which is what people mean when they refer to someone who "has backbone". You can develop "backbone" to deal with change and pressure in other parts of your life as you explore your full range of flexibility. Integrity of the spine can help create integrity of the mind. It is hard to think about anything else when you are breathing strongly in a strong backbend, so, by making the mind and body alert, backbends help combat depression and lethargy.

When we feel unsafe we instinctively fold in on ourselves. Bending backward counteracts this curling up and brings us out of our shelter. Lengthening and opening along the belly exposes our visceral organs, giving us practice in dealing with vulnerability. Backbends are like exploring uncharted territory. They allow us to practice spreading awareness to unfamiliar parts of the body. We never see our backs directly, needing instead to twist around to catch a reflection in a mirror. Bending backward is leaning into new terrain, requiring us to conquer the fear of the unknown.

In opening the heart center, backbends are enormously uplifting. The chest lifts and widens to encourage better breathing and full expansion of the lungs. Expanding the heart center uncramps, rejuvenates and welcomes joyful vitality into your life.

Always warm up with some standing postures before beginning backbends. To really feel your backbends develop, repeat the pose three times. The body does tend to feel the effects of holding backbends, so follow with some of the counter poses on page 81.

Those suffering from hypertension or heart trouble should work with an experienced teacher. Avoid strong backbends during menstruation, pregnancy and for eight weeks after giving birth. Anyone with a herniated disc, lumbar injury, peptic or duodenal hernia, as well as anyone who has recently had surgery, can practice mild backbends. If you find that weakness of the back or discomfort is present, build up your practice slowly and progressively.

Right: You must protect the vulnerable lower back and neck, making these parts stronger, and bring awareness to them.

About Alignment—*Special preparations for better backbends*

Stretch the legs and trunk and open the shoulders before backbending. Warm up the body with these exercises and your backbending will come more easily.

Neck Extension

Elongating the neck teaches you how to extend it in backbends without compressing the cervical spine.

1 Sit on your heels and drop your head back. Mentally visit your neck and observe how that feels. Notice how far back your gaze arrives as the head drops back.

2 Now interlace your fingers at the base of your skull. Close your eyes and take a moment to "grow" the neck, extending the crown of the head skyward. As you inhale, open your elbows out to the sides and back, and extend the neck so the back of your head moves away from your shoulders. Cradle your head so you keep the back of the neck long as you look up. If you measure where your gaze arrives, you may notice that there is not a large difference, yet more likely that this option feels better on your neck than the previous one. This feeling of the neck staying long is what you are aiming for in backbends like the Cobra and Locust Poses.

EXPLORE

If possible, from the Supta Virasana pictured opposite, come all the way down to lie on your back. To deepen the backbend, cup an elbow in each palm and take your arms overhead, bringing the elbows to touch the floor. Rest for up to several minutes, them release in Child Pose (see page 29).

Shoulder Extension

These shoulder exercises give more lift with "longer" released arms.

1 Stand side-on to the wall, at a distance of about 10in (25cm). The more flexible you are, the closer you will get to the wall. Stretch the arm closest to the wall as high up as you can reach, touching your palm to wall. Take several slow breaths, feeling like you are hanging down from the raised hand. Now take it back 45 degrees (pictured) for another 10 or so breaths. Finally, take it further behind, to be, if possible, parallel to the floor. Lean your chest forward and breathe. After doing one side, if you relax your arms and then swing them together to join the palms you might find the worked arm "longer" than the other. Repeat on the other side.

2 Bring your elbows to the padded edge of a table so they are shoulder-width apart. Step back so your ankles are under your hips and you form a table shape. Bring your palms together and lower the head, if possible, so the neck is in line with the spine. You will feel a stretch in the shoulders. This is table prayer pose. As you hold the position, let the side ribs soften down. After 10 breaths here, slowly lower your hands between your shoulder blades so your fingers point toward your tailbone. Move slowly between these two positions a few times. To come up, walk in, lift your head and scoop up.

Supta Virasana—*Reclining Hero Pose*

The ileopsoas is a deep muscle running from the inner thighbone to the lumbar vertebrae. When this muscle is tight or contracted, it pulls us into a forward bend. A released ileopsoas muscle is essential for healthy backbending. Begin in Virasana (see page 59). Lean back on your elbows, then come up a little so you can lift your pubic bone up as you stretch your tailbone away. Breathe here for a while. Maintaining the tilt of the pelvis, keep your floating ribs from jutting out as you lower your buttocks to the floor. Gaze straight ahead or take the head back and stretch the chin away. If this stretch is too strong on the thighs, practice the lunge outlined in the first part of Anjaneyasana (see page 74), and Virabhadrasana I (see page 47).

Anjaneyasana—*Crescent Moon Pose*

The ileopsoas-lengthening lunge part of this pose is a good warm-up for all the other backbends. There are two directions of movement of energy in this pose. The movement from the back of the waist down extends out through the back foot and allows the hips to descend. The upward stretch beginning at the waist radiates energy upward.

1 Kneel on a cushioned surface and step your left leg forward. Cup the floor with your fingertips and bring the hips forward to lunge. Ground through the back knee as you allow time and the breath to further open the left groin and descend the hips. Give the muscles time to relax in this pose. When you have connected to the grounding force of gravity and the hips have got the message to drop, lower the chest down slightly, lengthen forward with the breast bone, press the fingertips to the floor and lift up to increase the bend in the back. Then practice on the other side.

sink more to the floor. If the pressure of your back knee against the floor is uncomfortable, press down more through the top of the back foot. If you are comfortable and feel you have a good lifting sensation, proceed to the next step.

3 Lengthen the spine further, then lift the breastbone up, curve the back backward, and bring the shoulders and arms back. Drop the head back and stretch the chin away. Inhale to come out of the pose and repeat with the right leg forward.

2 Return to lunge on the first side. When you have followed the same steps, bring your hands to your front knee. Then, reach the arms forward and cross the fingers for strength. Lift the upper body up to the sky. Imagine that someone is gently pulling you by your wrists up out of your hips. At the same time, release the hips so that they

EXPLORE

The thoracic region bends back less easily than the lumbar and cervical regions. Remain aware of where you are working from when practicing backbends. Otherwise you will be at risk of overworking the lower back and neck and underworking the mid and upper back. Extend and arch the whole spine evenly to avoid compressing the spaces between the vertebrae.

Salabhasana—*Locust Pose*

This pose is very strengthening for the back. Due to the pressure on the abdomen it improves digestive function.

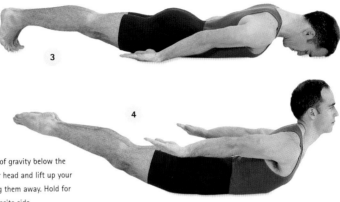

1 Lie face down with your forehead on the floor and your arms out in front of you. Have your arms and legs slightly apart. Slightly tilt your pelvis by pressuring your pubic bone to the floor. When you do this, you can reach your toes back further and the back of the waist lengthens.

2 Stretch your right arm and left leg away from each other. Tune into the opposite forces extending from your center of gravity below the navel to your toes and fingertips. Raise your head and lift up your right arm and left leg, continually stretching them away. Hold for several breaths before repeating on the opposite side.

3 After this warm-up, you are ready for Salabhasana. Bring your feet together and your arms by your sides. With your forehead on the floor, tuck your toes under, stretch your heels away and lift up your knees. Firm your thighs and keep both legs straight.

4 After several breaths, flick your toes away and lift your legs up in the air. Keep your inner ankles together. Re-anchor well through the pubic bone. Then lift your arms, head and chest up. Reach back with your fingers toward your toes to deepen the pose. Hold for five to ten breaths. Repeat three times.

After practicing Salabhasana, ease the lower back by turning your toes in toward each other and letting the heels flop out

to the sides. Make a pillow with your hands, turn your head to one side and rest for a while.

CAUTION

If you have a weak back, perform Salabhasana in segments. First, keep your upper body on the floor and lift one leg at a time, taking care to stretch it well back. When you have practiced with both sides, keep the feet on the floor and curl the upper body up, making sure you gather energy for the pose by lifting and reaching away with the arms.

EXPLORE

Lift from the entire lengthened spine, not by pivoting at one point at the waist. Visualize the spine moving in toward the center of the torso. Looking up with your eyes will help "lift" the body higher.

Bhujangasana—*Cobra Pose*

Though it might look simple, this pose requires determination and strength. Each time you take an inhalation, your abdominal organs benefit from the massage as your abdomen expands into the floor.

1 Lie face down with your forehead touching the floor and your feet together. Place your palms on the floor. Check that your fingertips don't creep past the line of your shoulders, but remain just underneath them so that your elbows are in the air. Use the following points to prepare yourself for maintaining healthy alignment once in the pose. Slide your shoulder blades down away from your ears toward your hips. Squeeze your elbows toward each other. Move your tailbone toward your feet and stretch your toes away to elongate the back.

2 Raise your hands 1in (2.5cm) off the floor, then lift your head, shoulders and chest. Mentally check in with the muscles of your back to feel which ones are working to hold you in place. Bring your hands back to the floor. Lengthen your tailbone and breastbone in opposite directions and then pressure your palms on the floor. Don't let this pose depend entirely on the strength of your arms. Use your arms to *assist*, but not override the work in the back. Most people will have their hips on the floor with arms well bent. Very flexible people may have straight arms. Hold for five to ten breaths. After three repetitions, use Child Pose (see page 29) or Downward-Facing Dog (see page 100) to release your back.

Incorrect x

Maintain the integrity of the pose. Don't hunch the shoulders or bend the elbows out to the side. Spread the stretch evenly through the spine and back of the neck rather than collapsing at the neck.

EXPLORE

From the shoulders down, the outer body encasing this central core moves down toward your toes. Visualize the inner body elongating with each breath. Your sternum lifts up like the "chest" of the cobra as you rise up to overcome any obstruction you face.

Ustrasana—*Camel Pose*

Forming the camel's hump strongly stretches the thighs, opens the groin and lifts the heart. The fifth chakra at the throat is activated in this posture where the head is tilted back and the chin stretched away.

1 Kneel (on a cushioned surface if you prefer) with your knees hip-width apart. Place your right hand on your lower back and stretch the other one straight up in the air. Push your hips forward and lift up the breastbone. Use the raised arm to give you a lift as you extend back. Keep the head and neck in line with the upper arm and breathe freely. Repeat on side two before sitting down on the heels.

2 While kneeling, tuck your toes under. This time, lift up well through the top arm and bring the other arm down so your fingers hold the heel. Don't twist the body. Keep both hips and front ribs facing forward. After five breaths, repeat on the other side.

3 Now you are warmed up for the full Ustrasana. From kneeling, take both hands to the small of your back and massage it a little. The energy moves down from the back of the waist to ground through the knees. Remember the feeling of lift that the raised arms gave to the first two exercises. Maintain the lift through the spine from the back of the waist upward to open the chest. Take the hands one by one to the heels. Then use them as your anchor to open the groin and stretch the hips forward, aiming to have the thighbones vertical. Continue to lift the breastbone to the sky as you roll your shoulders back. Finally, take your head back. When it is time to come up, pressure your feet on the floor, inhale and come up. After three repetitions, release the back by using Child Pose (see page 29).

1   2   3

EXPLORE

Increase the challenge of this pose by untucking the toes so the tops of the feet are on the floor. To further deepen the pose, bring the knees and feet together. Remember that both the front and back sides of the body must participate equally in the backbends. Exhale and soften the face to release tension.

Setu Bandhasana—*Bridge Pose*

Strengthen your body and expand your heart center in this pose.

1 Lie on your back with your knees bent up. Have your knees and feet body-width apart. Lift your pelvis slightly so your buttocks just begin to move off the ground. As you take several breaths in this position, lengthen your tailbone toward your feet. Now peel your vertebrae one by one off the floor. Tuck the shoulders under one by one and move the breastbone toward the chin.

2 A bridge reaches in both directions to the riverbanks. While the breastbone moves toward your chin, the tailbone moves toward the knees and the knees stretch away from you. Don't let your knees splay apart—keep them only as wide as your hips by squeezing the inner thighs toward each other. Check that excess tension is not building up in the neck. After holding five to ten breaths come down and rest. Repeat twice more. Then hug the knees into the chest and rock from side to side to release the back.

EXPLORE

If you can straighten your elbows, then interlace the fingers and press the arms down. If your body is ready for more of a challenge, grasp your ankles with your hands. Have patience as you approach each new edge in a pose. Respect the body and wait for it to let you in.

Matsyasana—*Fish Pose*

Matsyasana is a good pose for releasing the neck after practicing Shoulderstand, Plough and Knee to Ear Poses.

1 Sit on the floor with your legs in front. For this whole sequence you need to press the insides of the feet and thighs together. Lean back on your hands and pressure the palms to the floor. Lengthen the arms and lift up with the chest. Fully engage your mind in this process. Take your head back and don't forget to breathe. Lift the head and inhale as you come up out of the pose.

2 If you would like to take it a step further, lean back on your elbows so your fingers are by your buttocks. Press down into the elbows and lift the chest into a beautiful arch. With each inhalation, feel the spine move into the core of the body and elongate, setting it up for you to deepen the pose on the exhalation.

3 From position 2, slide your elbows apart to lower down on the crown of your head. Stretch your arms overhead, and reach the fingers away actively. To release, bring the arms to your sides, inhale to lift the head slightly, and then slide it away and lie flat.

EXPLORE

Bring your mental sensitivity to the back of the body; feel how it stretches and the skin thins out.

Urdva Dhanurasana—*Upward Facing Bow Pose*

Many people who have difficulty rising up into this pose assume that it is because they lack strength but often it is due to a lack of shoulder flexibility. If your shoulders are tight, then first practice releasing the shoulders with the table prayer pose from the section on alignment (see page 73). Prepare for this demanding pose with Crescent Moon Pose to open the groin and stretch the thighs.

1 Lie on your back, with your knees bent up. The action on the back is better when the feet are not turned out so check that your toes are pointing forward. Place your palms near the shoulders, fingers pointing in the direction of the hips. Hold here as you allow the anchoring of the heels to earth to take place. Fully feeling the weight of the heels, slowly peel the back up off the floor and lift the hips. Let the grounding of the body come through the heels, then down into the earth.

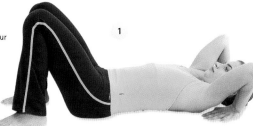

2 Watching the breath, wait for the inner cue to move. Catch it when it comes by lifting your hips as you pressure the palms and straighten the arms to lift into the full position.

3 Now that you are up, adjust your feet, which may have turned out. Press your inner thighs closer together. As in Bridge Pose, push the groin up. Let the spine move in toward the front of the body while you consolidate the pose, then expand it in both directions away from the back of the waist. It might help to lengthen toward the tailbone if you lift your heels off the ground for a few breaths.

CAUTION

This pose is not advisable in cases of slipped disc, hernia, heart problems and high blood pressure, during menstruation, pregnancy or in the post-natal period.

EXPLORE

Your yoga practice is not just how you look in a pose. It is how you are when you are not in it too. This includes going into and coming out of a pose. Never collapse out of a pose, but maintain a steady control. When resting in between repetitions, take your awareness to the back of the body (including the back of the brain) and you will recover more quickly.

After Backbending

Always practice a couple of twists and forward bends after a session on backbending.

Rocking

Your back will enjoy this massage. Lying down, hug your knees into your chest and rock slowly from side to side. Then press your knees away, resisting with your arms. More of your lower back will come into contact with the floor as you rock.

Janu Sirsasana *(see page 61)*

Janu Sirsasana nicely combines a forward bend with a twisting and lengthening action for each side of the back.

Sukhasana Twist *(see page 84)*

As the abdominal muscles contract in this twist, the muscles on the back side of the body can release.

Balasana—Child Pose *(see page 29)*
& Yogamudrasana *(see page 138)*
These two poses cultivate the sense of release and surrender.

Paschimottanasana *(see page 62)*

Stretch out the back and hamstrings in this pose.

Passive Reclining Twist *(see page 86)*
Let the softness inherent in this pose release the back.

Twists

From where you're sitting, twist around to one side for 10 breaths. Wind yourself up tight. Coil around with every cell in your torso. Now uncoil. Feel different? A twist is a great opportunity to turn and see things from a different angle.

When you feel wound up by life, temporarily increase the winding with a twist. Spiral up to the sky, then feel the tension dissipate as you undo and consciously unwind out of the twist.

The vertebrae are held in place by many small muscles and ligaments that need to be exercised to stay in top shape. Should they weaken, or should the distribution of strength through the back be uneven, the spine can be pulled out of alignment. A decrease of innervation can cause all sorts of problems in other areas and body systems.

An oft-used analogy is that of the dish sponge. When the sponge is full of soapy water, it can be squeezed out, ready to fill with clean water. That's what twists do to the abdominal organs. They temporarily increase the pressure on them so that the deoxygenated blood is squeezed out. Then the organs receive fresh oxygen and nutrient-rich blood.

Our well-being depends on a happy spine. Twists prevent stiffness of the spine and counteract any decrease in mobility that makes one look and feel old. Wringing out the body releases lots of built-up tension. Twists can reduce headaches and stiffness in the neck and shoulders. Depending on the cause, they can work miracles in relieving backache, as they stretch and strengthen the tiny muscles that link each vertebra to its neighbour. They help the spine maintain a healthy alignment.

Twists nourish the discs between the vertebrae. As the intervertebral discs have no direct blood supply from adulthood on, the bending forward, backward and twisting of yoga postures brings them the nutrients they need to keep healthy. When practicing twists, take some time to lengthen the torso first to be sure you are elongating, not compressing the spine.

Twists increase vitality, energy and boost the flow of prana around the body. By placing pressure on the organs of digestion, then releasing it, twists feed the digestive fire. Through their massaging effect on the organs, they eliminate sluggishness and ward off constipation.

Don't practice twists intensively if you have a hernia or have had recent surgery; consult an experienced teacher first. Proceed with extreme caution if you have disc problems, as the twists will need to be implemented gradually, allowing

Above: A twist offers a mental break and a time to view things from a fresh perspective.

for any delayed feedback from your body. Women benefit from practicing twists between periods to relieve menstrual cramps. During menstruation, use gentle twists. In pregnancy, practice simple twists in an open way (for example, without compressing the abdomen against the thigh) and flow in and out of them a few times without holding for long.

Pavritta Sukhasana—*Cross-Legged Twist*

Use this simple cross-legged pose to learn how to twist from bottom to top, and from inside to outside, with awareness.

1 Sit cross-legged and slide your feet crossways so the ankles align themselves under the knees. Bring the heels forward so your shinbones are more or less parallel with each other. Bring the fingertips of the right hand to cup the floor in front, and those of the left behind you.

2 The correct twisting action begins at the root of the back. Learn to work in segments to move the twist progressively up your spine so you can apply the same principles to other twists.

3 Pressure your fingertips down to the floor and inhale yourself taller. To begin the twist, visualize your abdominal organs twisting to the left and, on an exhale, activate the lower abdominal muscles so they move from right to left. On the next exhalation, shunt the middle abdominal muscles left. Visualizing an upward spiral of energy. Each time you inhale, feel a further lengthening upward of the spine, and on each exhalation, from the core of the body, twist deeper.

4 When you come to involve the chest in the twist, it works better to twist more on the *inhale*, rather than the exhale. Remembering to use at least one breath per section, turn the ribs more to the left, then bring the shoulders into the twist. Finally, turn your head left to find the position which feels right for your neck. Hold the pose for five to ten breaths, maintaining the feeling of spinning upward as you do so.

5 Unwind and take a moment to feel the effects that the twist has had on your body: sweep over your abdomen, ribs, back, shoulders and the rest of the body. Check in with your mind too. Twist to the other side, then change the way the legs are crossed and repeat.

3

X

Incorrect x

Don't jam the floating ribs forward as you bend the spine backward. Keep your back straight so your head and neck are over your pelvis. Both shoulders should be roughly the same height from the floor, as should both ears.

EXPLORE

The colon ascends on the right side and descends to the rectum on the left. Good intestinal functioning is encouraged by pressuring first one side and then the other.

Bharadvajasana I—*Sage Twist I*

Spiraling outward and upward releases tension from the whole torso.

1 From Dandasana, bring your legs around to the left and tuck the right foot under the left ankle. Have both knees facing forward. Hold your right knee with your left hand. Bring your right hand to the floor behind you. Sink the sitting bones toward the floor, and take as many breaths as you need to extend up from your base. If this starting position is not at all comfortable for you, place a small support like a cushion or folded blanket under one buttock to level yourself off.

2 When you have lengthened well, revolving from the hips, spiral into the fuller twist, moving with the support of your abdominal organs. If possible, slide your left hand under the knee, wrist facing out. Catch hold of your left arm with your right hand and look back over your shoulder. More advanced people can anchor down well through the left sitting bone, allowing the shortened left side of the waist to elongate as the right naturally does. After five to ten breaths, sit on your heels to rest and feel the effects, before repeating on side two.

EXPLORE

Bring your head into the pose just as you would normally. Measure with your eyes how far around you go. Now turn just your neck and head back to the front. This time, close your eyes, and, with awareness, bring your neck and head back around into the twist. Go only as far as feels healthily comfortable for your neck. Open your eyes and note how far you reached.

Jathara Parivartanasana—*Revolved Abdomen Pose*

Often weak abdominal muscles contribute to chronic back pain. This exercise, practiced daily, will quickly strengthen the muscles. The passive reclining twist is less strengthening, but wonderful for easing pain caused by tight back muscles pulling on the vertebrae and causing nerve irritation and pain.

Passive Reclining Twist

1 Lie on your back with your knees bent up close to the chest. Take your arms out to the sides. Keep your knees in close to the body and slowly drop both your knees over to the right side, aiming them toward your elbow. Relax both knees and feet down to the floor. If your knees or feet don't arrive there, rest them on a folded blanket. Turn your head to the left side. There is nothing more to do in this pose. Now bring your attention to actively undoing the parts of the body that are holding on to tension. Check the buttocks, back, shoulders and face. Stay in this pose for one to two minutes. To come up, turn your head back to center first, lift the top knee in the air, then the other leg, then proceed to side two.

2 Build toward the full pose with an intermediate exercise. Lie on your back with your arms out to the sides, hands at shoulder level. Bring both legs up in the air. Lift the hips and "bunny hop" the buttocks to the left. While extending out through both heels, hold the left leg steady and exhale your right leg out to the side, aiming your toes toward the fingertips. On your next exhalation, slowly lower your left leg to join the right. Inhale your left leg back to vertical and on your next inhalation, raise the right leg. Complete five repetitions on each side, following the flow of the breath. Bend your knees if necessary.

3

3 If your legs can come to at least a 90-degree angle then you are ready for the full pose with straight legs. If, when you raise your legs in the air, they don't come at least to vertical, keep your knees bent as you follow these instructions. "Bunny hop" your buttocks 6in (15cm) to the left, so that your toes angle off toward the right hand. Exhale to lower both legs to the right at the same time. If you can, catch hold of the feet. Your top heel will usually sit behind the other. To increase the twist, reach the top heel away as you "revolve" your abdominal muscles in the opposite direction. Anchor as much of the left side of your trunk and left shoulder to the floor as you can. Turn your head to gaze at your left hand. Do an even number of repetitions on each side, exhaling down and inhaling up. For the final repetition, stay in this twist for five breaths before inhaling up.

EXPLORE

You can move the emphasis of the passive twist up and down the back depending on where you place your knees. If your thighs are more at right angles with the torso, the emphasis of the twist is further down the back. If your knees start close to your chest and land close to your elbow, the twist moves up the back.

Passive Opening Out Twist

Stretching out like a starfish expands the heart. Open yourself to a childlike feeling of happiness.

1 Lie on your front with your arms and legs apart like a star. Your right hand and both your feet will stay attached to the floor, and your left arm will move.

1

2 As you bring your arm up and over, let your left hip come up. Allow your knees to bend gently and roll over more onto the sides of your feet. Turn the head to look behind you. Your left arm and shoulder might stay floating in the air. Either use gravity, patience and the breath to ease them down, or, if you like, rest them on a folded blanket. In time, gravity will assist the easing down process. If your left shoulder can touch the floor, stretch the other shoulder away to increase the distance between them.

2

3 Rest in this position for one to two minutes, tuning into the purity of the heart center. Before you move onto to do the same on the other side, rest like the starfish, or in Makrasana (see page 114) to observe what has been mobilized on the physical, mental and or emotional levels.

3

EXPLORE

In this position, one lung is more open than the other. Explore the expansion of the side ribs with each inhalation as the air is drawn more into that side of the chest and it is exercised fully.

Marichyasana III—*Sage Twist III*

This twist develops shoulder flexibility, tones the abdominal organs and stimulates sluggish intestinal function. This pose is named after Marichi, who, like Bharadvaja, was a man of great wisdom.

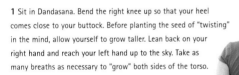

side of the torso as you do so. Follow the twisting principals from Pavritta Sukhasana (see page 84) to twist in sections from the base up. Feel yourself twisting from the inside out; from the inner organs to the outer casing of your body. Hold the pose for five to ten breaths, then untwist, re-center, and repeat on the other side.

1 Sit in Dandasana. Bend the right knee up so that your heel comes close to your buttock. Before planting the seed of "twisting" in the mind, allow yourself to grow taller. Lean back on your right hand and reach your left hand up to the sky. Take as many breaths as necessary to "grow" both sides of the torso.

2 This next part is crucial. You need to lean forward and wedge your left elbow to the right outer knee *without* losing the length you have just gained. Do this movement consciously, over one or more exhalations, taking care not to shorten the right

3 For the full posture, straighten your right arm forward. Reach well forward as if you were taking your armpit beyond the right outer knee. From the shoulder, rotate the whole arm so that the thumb turns down, and wrap your arm around the right knee. Clasp the left wrist behind your back, or work your hands toward each other using a soft belt. As you breathe deeply in this pose, the pressure of your thigh against your abdomen gives the organs a healthy massage.

EXPLORE

The breath tends to shorten and feel more labored in this twist. Consciously smoothe and round out the breath.

Balances

Our lives feel better when they are well balanced. We are healthiest when we find the appropriate balance in our food and we feel best when we find the right levels of activity and sleep. Intellectual balance means we are able to see both sides of the coin, and be less judgmental.

Emotionally, we seek to lessen extremes of emotions, decrease mood swings and be more even-tempered. Spiritual balance lets us keep higher ideals in mind as our actions create our lives, yet still allows us to keep our feet on the ground. A spiritual belief balances and gives meaning to our physical existence. Being out of balance is a huge source of stress and tends to create problems. Your yoga practice is a metaphor for your life. Finding your balance in a pose is practice at finding your balance in your life. Yoga, as a re-harmonizer, helps you move closer to your own perfect balance.

Balance poses convey self-sufficiency. Standing on your own two feet does more than just develop the small muscles of the ankles. Balancing poses allow us to explore our connection with our base. In India, the lotus flower is a powerful symbol. The white flower is a symbol of purity.

It floats on top of its stem, a long taproot that is anchored in deep, dark waters. Like the lotus flower, we sink our roots into the earth, and soar skyward. Balance poses allow you to connect to your roots and explore whether they feel strong, independent and able to support your growth.

Some poses look simple but actually present a real challenge. All balance poses require that the mind and body work together. The focused mind collaborates with the grounded body. Aside from developing concentration and stamina, the poses develop patience. Don't be in a hurry. Decide for how many breaths you will stay in the pose, then stay. If you come out early, keep a quiet mind, and bring yourself back into it again.

Arm balances develop endurance. They work the shoulder girdle, which helps balance out office-bound people. By building strength in the upper body, they

redistribute tension in a healthy way, which helps decrease neck tension. Developing the arms enables us to reach out in life, either to take what we need or to give what we can.

Balance poses teach us about relaxing in all the other postures. Try balancing when holding your body tight. It will feel very different from when you proceed in a soft, easy manner that brings a lightness into your pose. Use the skeleton rather than tensed muscles to support you. As your

Above: Being out of balance creates stress. Yoga practice helps you move closer to a balanced way of living.

mind stays calm and centered and develops the ability to lead the body, your coordination will grow. Developing physical poise will foster mental harmony.

Utthita Hasta Padangusthasana—*Hand to Foot Pose*

When a balance pose is a challenge to flexibility, it is amazing how we are forced to focus to stay up. This is good practice.

1 Stand in Tadasana (see page 43) and ground yourself through your heels. Quieten the mind so that you can fully focus on what you are doing right here and now: this balance. Gaze at a fixed point at eye level. Bend the right knee slightly and pause to let your left leg better connect with the earth. Lift up your right leg and hold the knee with your right hand. With your left hand to your hip, lift the sternum so your posture stays erect. Lengthen the right side waist by moving the right hip down level with the left. Pressing the knee closer to the torso, hold for seven even breaths.

2 Now open the leg out to the right. Roving eyes will distract you by taking your awareness elsewhere. Turn your head to gaze left and keep your eyes steady. If you are holding your knee, lift it toward your armpit. If you are holding your toe (see alternative), lift it as high as you can. Keep the supporting leg straight. Breathe here for seven rounds. Then, still balancing, bring the leg back to the front. Release the leg and straighten it in mid-air. Lower the leg slowly and practice the other side.

Alternative A

If your hamstrings are flexible, loop your big toe with the thumb and finger and straighten the leg out in front. Now keep both sides of the torso an even length by rolling the outer right hip down with an external rotation of the thigh bone.

CAUTION

During pregnancy, practice standing balances near a wall so there is no risk of falling.

1

2

A1

A2

EXPLORE

To build hamstring flexibility, stand in front of a table and place your heel on it. Level the hips by lowering the raised leg side.

Garudasana—*Eagle Pose*

This pose develops concentration and coordination and is wonderful for tight shoulders.

1 Standing in Tadasana become aware of the skin on the soles of the feet as the feet widen out against the floor. Move your attention to the pressure of the right foot against the floor. Quietly let the skin of the foot melt down into it. Then bend the left knee and lift up the right leg.

2 Use momentum to wrap the right leg around the left leg. If you have difficulty with this, bend the supporting leg more. If possible, keep the top knee facing forward, not turned outward. To wrap the arms, hug yourself with your left arm on top of the right. Keeping the cross at the elbows, bring the backs of the hands toward each other, then cross wrist and forearm to bring the palms together.

3 Lift the elbows up so they rise off the chest and free breath is not impeded. To stretch into the shoulders more, ease your forearms forward so your thumbs move away from your nose. Let your eagle fold forward, as if looking down on the world from a great height. When you breathe deeply, you will feel the skin between the shoulder blades stretch on each inhalation. Hold the pose for 10 breaths, before unwrapping, re-grounding and repeating on the opposite side.

1

2

EXPLORE

Feel free to practice the upper and lower body movements independently, before uniting them in Garudasana.

Virabhadrasana III—*Warrior III*

Let your warrior-like determination give you a mental surge to charge the body with energy.

1 Assume the pose for Virabhadrasana I with your right foot forward (see page 47).

2 Inhale deeply and, on the exhalation, fold your torso over your front leg, lowering your ribs toward your thigh. On a strong inhalation, straighten the right leg and lift the back leg up to parallel with the floor. Gaze straight ahead. Keeping your right leg straight, lower your left hip down so it is even with the right. Turn your left toes from the side down toward the floor and extend back through the heel. (You can even place your hands on the back of a chair to practice the alignment.) Visualize a line of energy running along the body. From the back of the waist it extends forward, reaching out toward the fingertips. From your center, it extends backward through the back heel, so everything from heel to fingertips unkinks and elongates. Hold the pose for five breaths before coming gracefully back to Virabhadrasana I.

EXPLORE

Before coming into a pose, close your eyes and visualize yourself clearly in a strong, stable, steady pose.

Navasana—*Boat Pose*

We can learn the most from the asanas we find the most challenging. By practicing Navasana daily you will notice an increase in abdominal strength within a few weeks.

1 From Dandasana, lean back onto your hands, and tilt the pelvis forward. Feel how the vertebral column moves upward and in toward the front of the body. The muscles in the lower back and along the spine engage and the chest lifts. When the stomach muscles work, the belly will naturally bulge a little. However, use this pose to practice an internal energy lock called Uddyana Bandha. Apply this lock by tucking in your lower abdomen, just above the pubic bone and below the navel so it draws closer toward your spine. As you lift your toes in the air, this sucking inward will stop any bulging in the lower abdomen. To go a step further, raise your legs in the air. Practice keeping the inward curve in the lower back, chest lifted and sucking in of the lower abdomen to stop it bulging. Repeat three times, holding for five long breaths.

Alternative

To move to a more challenging option, have the knees bent so that the shins are parallel to the floor. Without rounding the back or collapsing the chest, reach the arms toward the toes.

2 In the final pose, keep in mind the principles you practiced initially. Straighten your legs in the air. Adhere the front thigh muscles to the thigh bones, as if they were to tuck up into the torso. This will give you a lift to help prevent any sinking of the chest. Without rounding the back or collapsing the chest, reach your hands forward and gaze up at your big toes.

EXPLORE

If your back is strong, you can lie on your back with arms overhead and lift up into the final pose in a single movement.

Bhujapidasana—*Arm Pressure Balance*

Despite appearances, this pose doesn't require more upper body strength than you already have. Technique is all-important. With attention to proper positioning and a positive mental attitude you will be well on your way to balancing.

1 Stand with the feet hip-width apart. As you fold forward, bend the knees but keep your hips high in the air. Take the right arm through the legs and around the right leg. A common error is not to take the whole arm—up to the shoulder—through the legs. It is important that the back of the thigh contacts as high up the upper arm as possible so use your other hand to stabilize you if necessary. Place the right palm flat on the floor just next to the right foot with fingers facing forward. Now take the left arm through to bring that palm flat to the floor. You'll need to keep the hips high so you don't squash your upper arm and get stuck halfway in, unable to proceed.

2 Bending your elbows well, lean forward. Inch your feet together and forward. Lift up through the abdominal region (see bandhas on page 95) and raise your head to gaze forward. Shift your weight to transfer more weight to the palms as you lift your feet up in the air to cross the ankles. Straighten the arms and hold for five to ten breaths. After resting, repeat with the feet crossed the opposite way.

1

2

EXPLORE

Should your wrists need strengthening, practice Adho Mukha Svanasana (see page 100). To counterstretch the arms after Bhujapidasana, Bakasana or Adho Mukha Svanasana, kneel and place the backs of the hands on the floor, fingers facing toward your knees. Move the hips back about 2in (5cm). Feel the welcome release along the wrists and forearms as you lean back.

Bakasana—*Crane Pose*

This pose, resembling a bird, strengthens the upper body and abdomen.

1 Squat with your feet together. Place your hands on the floor as wide as your shoulders, middle fingers facing forward. Bend your knees to rest them high up the upper arms, wrapping your inner knees around the upper arms. Bring the feet together and come onto your tiptoes.

2 Lean forward to allow the transfer of weight from toes to palms. Gaze forward along the floor. Lift the abdominal muscles and use yogic energy locks, the bandhas (see page 95), to give your body lift and lightness. One at a time, or together, raise the feet toward the buttocks. Keep your abdominal muscles contracted to help draw the legs into the body. Straighten your arms. Take five breaths before coming down with control.

1

2

EXPLORE

As you commit to a pose, you agree to go on a journey and appreciate what it has to offer you. When practicing balancing poses, decide first for how many breaths you will stay, and keep to it.

Inversions

Holding a position with a whole new

relationship to gravity demands a certain

steadiness of posture and mind. Inversions

develop confidence and help quiet the

brain in times of stress.

Inversions are key poses for regaining hormonal balance, as better blood circulation tones the endocrine glands. In particular, Headstand tones the pituitary and pineal glands in the brain, both of which have wide-ranging effects in the body. Shoulderstand and Plough Pose bring blood to the thyroid and parathyroid glands by the throat.

The lymphatic system, involved in immune support and clearing toxins from the tissues, reaps the benefits from anti-gravity positions. The lymphatic vessels don't have any valves or muscles to help pump their fluid through. The passive flow instead relies on changes in position and massaging movements from the muscles surrounding them. Going upside down helps drain toxins

Inverted poses clear the head and help concentration. The brain receives an increased blood supply, combating tiredness and lethargy.

from the extremities down toward their destination, the lymph nodes. The lymphatic fluid drains in the direction of the heart, and, by assisting this process, inverted poses help to relieve strain or swelling in the legs and clear the path for better circulation of the blood.

Inversions are even considered aerobic, as the heart must pump harder to pump out the more rapidly filling ventricles. The functioning of the organs is stimulated by the change in position and circulation, and intestinal laziness is lessened by the alteration in internal pressure.

When you feel stuck, or in need of inspiration, it helps to see the world from another angle. Releasing the pressure of our normal reality—gravity—can lighten the mind too.

An upside-down position is an opportunity to consider things from a different point of view. Apart from being mentally revitalizing and rejuvenating, inversions have the same physical action. By cleansing and nourishing the tissues, many people swear by their effects at maintaining youthfulness. As a sort of holistic beauty treatment, they might be the closest you can get to turning back the clock.

If you suffer high blood pressure, a neck problem, eye, ear or sinus problems, heart problems, hiatus hernia or dizzy spells, seek advice from a medical practitioner or experienced yoga teacher before beginning inversions.

During pregnancy, work with an experienced teacher. Inversions are not normally advisable during menstruation, as they tend to slow the flow of blood. Don't practice inverted poses if you have a headache at the time. As inversions are considered to be both calming to the mind and cooling to the system, they are generally used toward the end of your asana practice, and when your body has been warmed by the other poses.

Below: Going upside down helps cleanse and nourish the tissues. The overall effect is rejuvenating.

Adho Mukha Svanasana—*Downward-Facing Dog*

This is an excellent pose for stretching and strengthening the whole body. This forward-folding mild inversion is useful to link standing poses. Although it may not feel very restful at first, it can become so when you develop strength and flexibility. If, instead of being relatively straight, your back rounds in the full Downward-Facing Dog, practice Puppy Dog. As a gentler way to open the shoulders, you can hold and breathe in this pose longer. If wrist problems prevent you doing the full pose at this time, begin with this easier version.

1 Begin on all fours with your hands placed about 6in (15cm) in front of the shoulders. Check that the middle finger is pointing straight ahead, and spread the fingers wide.

1

2

2 Have your knees and feet body width apart. Tuck the toes under and lift up to an inverted "V" position. On tiptoes, bend both knees deeply, so your ribs come toward the thighs, or even touch. You will feel an increase in the stretch through the shoulders and an opening in the chest. At the same time, lift the sitting bones as the buttocks stay high and tilt the pelvis forward. The inward curve in the lower back will deepen as your navel moves closer to your thighs. (This pose is also a forward bend, so refresh your body's memory about folding from the hips: see page 49.) You will feel the muscles along the spine working strongly and get a lifting sense of elongation along the spine.

3 Keeping the hips at the same height, *slowly* straighten the legs. If the hips stay at, or nearly at, the same height, everything in between will need to lengthen. Practice this several times, with full awareness, so you don't lose the feeling of height or the inward curve in the lower back. To complete Downward-Facing Dog, swivel your feet so the outside edges of your feet are parallel—the inner heels will be further away from each other than the big toes. Stretch your heels toward the ground (until you develop a lot of flexibility along the backs of the legs, they will remain in the air). Distribute the pressure equally through the whole palm and fingers. Widen the space between the earlobes and upper arms by turning the outer edges of the armpits in toward each other. Hold for 10 to 15 breaths. Rest in Child Pose (see page 29) afterward. Soften the arms from the shoulders all the way to the wrists. To release the wrists, follow the instructions on page 96.

Alternative—*Puppy dog*   A

This gentler version of Downward-Facing Dog gives the shoulders a good stretch. Kneel on the floor. Place your hands far forward and lower your forehead to the floor. Have your knees under your hips so your buttocks are high in the air, not near the heels. From the back of the waist, extend back strongly through the tailbone. At the same time direct your energy from the waist forward through the arms.

Alternative—*Raised Leg Variation*   A

To make this pose into a stronger inversion, start with your feet together. Turn the right toes out and lift the right leg high up in the air. Keep both shoulders level. Let your right hip rise up and extend back through both heels. After five to ten breaths, lower the leg and stretch through both legs (or rest in Child Pose) before practicing the other side.

EXPLORE

Remember that yoga is not just doing postures and your yoga practice doesn't have to end here. Integrate yoga into your life by going about your daily life with awareness and consciousness.

Sirsasana—*Headstand* / Sasankasana—*Hare Pose*

Your head weighs about 9lb (4kg), your body considerably more. Your neck can hold the weight of your head only when you are properly prepared. It is essential to understand the lifting through the shoulders and pay due attention to alignment. This is not a beginners' pose and I strongly recommend you ask an experienced teacher to observe your alignment. If Headstand is not yet for you, the Hare pose is a possible alternative.

Headstand is a yogic icon, often the first pose people think of when they first hear of yoga. Ironically, you must get your head out of the way in Headstand. If you want to do this classic pose just because your ego wants to do "real yoga", it doesn't necessarily mean your body is ready to follow.

Practice Headstand well into your practice when your body is warm. Before going up, visualize yourself in the posture. Form a clear picture of yourself in a steady, stable pose.

1 Always practice Headstand on a cushioned surface like a folded blanket. Place your blanket in front of a wall, or in the corner of two walls. Kneel in front of your blanket. To measure out the correct elbow width, place your forearms on the blanket, and cup each elbow in the opposite hand. Your elbows should be not wider than your shoulders. Then form your triangle of support by interlacing your fingers together. Your knuckles should be 2in (5cm) from the wall.

2 When performing a safe Headstand, it is crucial to lift well from elbows to shoulders. Tuck your toes under and straighten your knees so you are in an inverted "V" shape. Practice your lift by pressing down through the elbows and moving the shoulders up toward the hips. This movement should increase the distance between the shoulders and earlobes as well as lifting the head away from the floor. If you find you can't lift your head away from the floor, you are not ready for Headstand yet. You need to develop your shoulder flexibility and/or strength before attempting to go up into Headstand. For shoulder flexibility, practice the shoulder exercises on page 72, as well as Gomukhasana (see page 68), and Garudasana (see page 93). To develop arm strength, practice Downward-Facing Dog (see page 100).

3 Take your knees back to the floor and position your head on the floor to be cupped by your interlaced fingers. For the correct alignment in the neck, it is the crown of the head that should be in contact with the floor. Once again raise the knees off the floor and practice moderating the pressure on the head. Ground down through the elbows, distribute weight into the edges of the hands against the floor, lift the shoulders up toward the hips. If you are not able to minimize the pressure on the crown of the head with these actions, then don't move onto the next step. Develop this skill with more preparatory work before you come up into Headstand.

4 If you have passed these checks, then walk your feet in as much as possible. There will come a point where the feet naturally want to lift. Lift them with knees bent so your heels come near your buttocks. Don't raise the legs all the way up straight away. Follow these steps to help your alignment stay true. Lift up from your elbows through your shoulders to your hips once more.

5 If you are not using a wall and you feel balanced, keep your knees bent and raise the thighs so that the knees point upward. Your heels will still be near your buttocks as you do this. Then straighten your legs up. If you are by a wall, straighten your legs and lift upward through the balls of the feet.

5

6

6 Check that your floating ribs are not jutting out—lengthen the back of the waist to bring them in. Should your shoulders be collapsing and causing the head to bear more than a little pressure, come down immediately. Energize the back of the body too. In the beginning hold for five breaths. Over many months, slowly build your holding time to up to five minutes. Come down by reversing the steps you took to go up. Always rest in Child Pose afterward and follow on with Shoulderstand.

A

Headstand, Shoulderstand, Halasana and Karnapidasana should not be practiced during menstruation or with some ear or eye problems, like detached retina or glaucoma. For heart problems, high blood pressure, previous neck injuries or pregnancy, seek the advice of an experienced teacher.

Alternative—_Hare pose_   A
(If Headstand if not yet for you, this is a possible alternative).
Begin in Child Pose (see page 29). Hold the sides of your feet with your hands. Lifting the buttocks high, inhale and roll over your head onto the crown. On the exhalation, release back to Child Pose. Repeat five times.

Sarvangasana—*Shoulderstand*

This hormonal balancing and deeply calming pose is well worth practicing daily.

1

2

1 To enable you to keep your neck relaxed in this pose, fold two or three blankets to the size that will support your base. Place the folded edges neatly one on top of the other. Lie over them with your head on the lower level, and the tops of your shoulders on your blankets, 2in (5cm) from the edge.

2 With control, bring your legs and hips in the air and then support your back. If your stomach muscles are not yet strong enough to bring you up, or if you can't yet come up in a well-controlled way that feels safe, use the wall method. Once you are up, bend your knees toward your head. Take several breaths to settle your shoulders into the pose. Let yourself come more onto the tips of the well-grounded shoulders and walk the hands down your back. Finally, stretch your legs up into the air. In the beginning, your legs may be angled to be quite bent overhead, not straight up in the air. Bring your elbows closer together. You may get a better grip holding your palms against the skin on your back rather than your clothes. In time, work on lessening the crease where the thighs join the torso. Visualize a line of energy from the inner thigh to the inner heel.

3 Never turn the head from side to side in this pose. Shoulderstand is not called neckstand for good reason! Although it might look like the neck is taking a lot of weight, the neck muscles need to stay relatively soft. If possible, ask a friend to touch the muscles on either side of your neck to check they are not strained tight. Likewise, redness or strain in the face means it's time to come down and rest. Build your time in the pose from one to up to 10 minutes.

4 After Shoulderstand, you can practice Halasana or Karnapidasana (pages 106 and 107). To come down, use the abdominal muscles to lower yourself down in a slow, controlled way. Slide off the blankets and lie flat. Release your neck by turning your head from side to side. The lower back and abdominal organs will probably communicate some different sensations to you, so practice with a twist and a forward bend afterward. A nice sequence starts with Matsyasana to release the neck. Then hug your knees to your chest and rock slowly from side to side. Follow with Passive Reclining Twist (see page 86) and Janu Sirsasana (see page 61), which work wonderfully after Shoulderstand. Finally practice Paschimottanasana (see page 63) and finish with Savasana (see page 30).

1

2

For contraindications
to Shoulderstand,
see page 103.

Shoulderstand Against the Wall

This controlled, step-by-step way of lifting into Shoulderstand in stages is a good way to start feeling comfortable with Shoulderstand.

1 Place your folded blankets a little away from the wall—as your head needs to be off the blankets but your shoulders supported by them, you may have to experiment to find the correct width for the length of your body. If you have a non-slip yoga mat, place it on top of the blankets. Sit side on and up close to the wall. Using your arms for support, slowly bring your legs up the wall and move your trunk around and down until you are lying over the blankets.

2 If you have found the right position with your blankets, your head will be on the floor, your shoulders 2in (5cm) from the edge of the blankets and your buttocks near the wall. Lift your head and check that your body is symmetrical, perpendicular to the wall.

3 Now you are ready to come up! With knees bent, press your feet into the wall and lift your hips. Hold your back and straighten yourself up by moving your hips more in line over your shoulders. If you like, you can straighten each leg in turn bringing one foot up the wall. Once you have both legs straight against the wall, take one leg, then the other, overhead and away from the wall. Come down by reversing the steps you took to go up.

3

EXPLORE

A few variations keep the mind alert in Shoulderstand. Practice lowering down one foot to the floor while keeping the leg extending strongly upward. Alternatively, bring the soles of the feet together and open the knees out in a kind of upside-down Cobbler's Pose. Follow that by opening your legs into a wide V shape.

Halasana—*Plough Pose*

If you are comfortable in Shoulderstand, follow on with this soothing pose. It has similar effects and contraindications to Shoulderstand.

1 From Shoulderstand lower your legs overhead. You need to be careful not to overstretch the neck as you bring your toes to touch the floor. If you are not able to bring your toes to the floor, then rest them on a higher surface, such as a chair placed a couple of feet behind the head. (If your toes are not supported, then continue to support your back with your hands.)

2 Once your toes are resting on a surface, stretch your arms along the floor. This will help you roll more onto the tips of your shoulders and deeper into this upside-down forward bend. Interlace your fingers and deepen the pose by stretching your arms and legs in opposite directions. Gradually build up until you can hold this pose for five minutes. Make Plough Pose more restful by supporting the thighs with a chair (see page 115).

3 Roll out of the pose with control, using your abdominal muscles to lower both legs until you are lying flat. See Shoulderstand for complementary asanas to follow on with.

Rollings—*From Halasana to Paschimottanasana*
You can enjoy a lovely massage for the muscles along the spine by rolling between Halasana and Paschimottanasana. If you are very comfortable in Plough Pose, lie on a cushioned surface, and use a little momentum and a lot of abdominal strength to roll slowly between these two positions. Inhale as you roll up and back to Halasana and exhale as you roll forward to Paschimottanasana.

Karnapidasana—*Knee to Ear Pose*

Withdraw into a fetal position after practicing Shoulderstand and Plough Pose.

If you feel comfortable in Halasana, practice this deep forward stretch by cushioning yourself with a couple of folded blankets and bending your knees beside your head. If your knees and tops of the feet don't come to the floor, place your legs on raised supports or tuck your toes under if necessary. To deepen the pose, straighten both arms along the floor and interlace your fingers. If your knees touch the floor, fold your arms over the backs of your knees. Hold this pose for 10 to 20 breaths before coming back to Halasana.

For contraindications to Halasana and Karnapidasana, see page 103.

Dynamic Yoga

The Sun Salutation is a group of postures that flow together to warm the body and work the heart. While you link movement and breath, you stretch and strengthen the muscles, developing stamina, coordination and confidence. There are many possible variations of Surya Namaskar to suit all ages and abilities so ask your teacher for help if necessary.

9 Inhale and step the right leg between your hands.

8 Downward-Facing Dog Exhale while you tuck your toes under and lift the hips high. Hold for three breaths.

7 Cobra Lower your body to the floor, then inhale as you press your hands to the floor to curve the chest up in Cobra Pose.

The sun is a symbol of the inner light that is in all of us. The bowing is an exercise of deep respect for this shining light; the folding and unfolding movements a tribute to creation. As you develop a graceful flow of one movement per breath, these linked postures become a moving meditation. Start your practice with three rounds and build to six, offering up each one like a prayer. Afterwards sit quietly and listen as your body tells you what it would like to practice next.

EXPLORE

Give yourself time to feel your way into the poses by holding each one for several slow breaths. Practice Ujjayi breathing (see page 131) during the Sun Salutation.

Surya Namaskar—*Sun Salutation*

10

11

1

12

START

1 Mountain Pose With palms together, ground through the feet and feel the connection with the earth through the soles of the feet.

2 Inhale your arms skyward As the front of your torso lengthens, keep the back side of the torso long as well.

3

2

10 Intense Forward Stretch
Exhale as you step your left leg forward to fold over your legs. If your legs are straight, press your hands more to the floor.

11 Switch on your thigh muscles and those of the lower abdomen as you inhale skyward. Lift everything from the hips up, except the shoulders.

FINISH

12 Exhale and bring the arms down to Mountain Pose ready to repeat on the left side.

3 Intense Forward Stretch
Exhale and fold forward to touch the earth.

6

4 With fingertips touching the floor (bend your knees if necessary) lunge. Inhale and step your left leg back. Lift your chest away from your thighs.

4

6 Still exhaling, bring your shoulders forward of your wrists, so your elbows form a right angle as you lower your body to 2in (5cm) off the floor.

5 Exhale and step your feet back to plank pose, forming a straight line from heels to shoulders.

5

Restorative Yoga

Restorative poses open the body, yet allow the nervous system to rest. Though you can still stretch deeply, the support helps you feel safe and comfortable yielding to the pose, and you can stay in it for longer. It enables you to recharge by expending minimal energy.

A s such, these poses are wonderful should you need to build energy stores during a chronic illness or to tap into your inner reserves and rejuvenate whenever you feel depleted. Savasana relaxation (see page 30), Child Pose (see page 29), Discovering the Breath (see page 128) and letting yourself hang down in the Roll Downs (see page 38) are also restorative practices. Incorporate restorative poses into your regular practice routine, either by practicing them a few days each month (they are ideal during menstruation), or by bringing one or two poses into each more active practice session. To find props around your house, think creatively and use sofa cushions, cushions, blankets, chairs, soft belts and bathrobe ties. Using an eyebag helps to give the system a break from sensory overload.

Supta Konasana—*Supported Angle Pose*

This pose creates space in the pelvis, eases menstrual dysfunction and supports the digestive system. It is worth folding a pile of soft, warm blankets to enable you to luxuriate in complete comfort in this pose.

Use a bolster or fold up several blankets so that they are longer than your torso. Sit at one end of your support and bring the soles of your feet together, heels toward your groin. Lie back over the bolster and have an extra cushion under your head so that it is higher than the heart. Let your knees fall out to the sides and use pillows or folded blankets of equal heights to support your thighs. Find the right balance between opening the hips and staying comfortable—if the stretch becomes too intense it will be hard to rest. Cover your body for warmth if necessary. Lay your arms out to the sides, palms facing up. If your elbows don't naturally reach the floor, then fold towels or blankets to support the forearms. Close or cover your eyes and rest for five to ten minutes. When you come up, stretch forward in Child Pose, or a variation of it with your big toes together, knees apart and arms stretched forward.

Forward Bend with a Chair

The same principle can be used for many forward bends: Trianga Mukhaikapada Paschimottanasana, Janu Sirsasana, Ardha Baddha Padma Paschimottanasana, Paschimottanasana and Baddha Konasana.

Sit on the edge of a folded blanket with your legs wide apart. Place a second blanket over the seat of a chair. Bring the chair far enough away so that when you fold forward your forehead will rest on it. To keep the chest open, bring the arms up to hold the chair base or back—experiment to find the most comfortable position. If you feel too much stretch, use cushions to raise the level of your forehead. After some time in the pose, your body will release and you'll find you can slide the chair further away to deepen the stretch. If you are very flexible, then you can rest your forehead on just a bolster or cushions. The gentle pressure on the forehead rests the frontal lobe of the brain, helping to quieten the mind and soothe the soul. Next, in this resting variation of Upavista Konasana, you can do two twists too. Turn your torso to face over one leg, position the chair over it and fold forward to rest the forehead. Hold each forward bend for one to two minutes.

Viparita Karani—*Restorative Inversion*

Viparita Karani, as a mudra (see page 138), is used to seal life energy in your body. Enjoy the benefits of an inversion without the effort of holding yourself in place. To relieve swelling in the legs after a hard day, or to ease the pain of varicose veins, practice for 10 minutes every day. During menstruation, forgo the blankets and simply lie on the floor with the legs up the wall.

Take a bolster or fold several blankets and place them by a wall. To come into the position, sit on your prop and lie yourself down on your side so your buttocks stay high and near the wall. Roll onto your back and take your legs up the wall. Check your position. Your abdomen needs to be parallel to the floor and your rib cage will curve downward. You may need to experiment a bit to get the right height and width in your blankets. If either is wrong, it will feel like you might slide off and you won't be able to relax properly. When the position feels perfect, look along your body to check that your trunk is perpendicular to the wall. If you like, tie a soft belt around the mid thighs so your legs don't have to work to hold their position. You can cover your eyes with an eye bag. Choose a comfortable arm position— either slightly away from your sides with your palms facing up, or with the arms overhead and elbows softly bent. Rest and breathe.

Makrasana—*Crocodile Pose*

This resting position has a gentle backbend so it is useful for resting without breaking the flow in between stronger backbends. Experiment to find the angle of the upper arms that will give you the perfect feeling of the right amount of backbend and the right angle for the resting neck and head.

Lie face down with your feet wide apart and toes turned out. Cup each elbow in the opposite hand and slide the forearms away so they are a short way in front of your shoulders. Lower your head to rest your forehead down on your forearms. Each time you inhale, your abdomen will expand down into the earth. Become attuned to the soothing sensation of this massage. This position is also useful to enable you to feel the expansion and consolidation along the back of the torso with each breath.

EXPLORE

A forward-bending restorative pose which also creates a belly massage and permits the expansion of the back ribs is Child Pose (page 29).

Salamba Halasana—*Supported Plough Pose*

A low table or a chair with space in its backrest for you to put your legs through can be the perfect prop. For when to avoid this pose, refer to Sirsasana (see page 103).

From Halasana (see page 106), rest your thighs on a hip-high support. Bring the legs of your prop in near the shoulders. It must be very close to the body as, for you to be able to fully relax, it is vital that the root of the thighs be fully supported. If your support is not high enough, then place folded blankets on top to raise it. Place your arms along the floor, or, if the chair legs allow it, take the arms overhead, elbows bent to about 90 degrees. Rest in this pose for two to five minutes. When you come down, lie on a flat surface and rest for a while.

EXPLORE

Expand your breath awareness from the asanas into your life. Whenever your phone rings, take three full breaths before you answer. (Place a note on your handset to remind you.) You'll surely set yourself up for a more pleasant conversation.

Yoga on a Chair

These make great office exercises and they are useful for the elderly or infirm. If you are at work, shut the door and take your phone off the hook to give yourself the best chance for full mental relaxation.

Centering

Sit comfortably on your chair. Have your feet well anchored to the ground. Bring the backs of your hands to your thighs. Sit with your back erect so you are not leaning against the backrest. Let your arms and shoulders relax and have your chin parallel to the floor. With each inhalation observe the expansion of the abdomen, ribs and chest. The whole torso is alive with the gentle pulsation of the breath. Even the back of the body opens up, then softens inward rhythmically. Raise the inhalation from the back of the waist, upward. Each time you exhale feel the natural, passive release. As all heavy thoughts float away, the head will lighten so it feels like it floats happily on the top of your spine. The more you practice this, the quicker you will learn to re-center. Practise centering whenever you can throughout the day, letting your tensions drift away as you return to your true, peaceful inner self.

Backbend

Different chairs will give you stretches of various intensities at different points along the spine, so experiment with a few to find the best one for you. The chair back should be below or level with the lower part of your shoulder blades. If your chair is high-backed, sit on telephone books to raise your seat. Lift out of your hips and lean back over your chair. Let your head move back as you stretch your chin away. You can, if you prefer, sit with your back to the wall and find a comfortable angle to rest your head against the wall so that you are completely relaxed.

Take the arms overhead and stretch them away like two rays of energy to expand the backbend and make this stretch more invigorating. Take care that you do not slump—keep each vertebra actively lifting away from the one below it. Take five to ten chest-opening breaths.

Twist

Sit with your left hip to the back of the chair. Have your knees and feet hip-width apart. Rest your feet on a support if they don't easily meet the ground. Raise your arms straight up in the air. Let your torso rise out of your hips. Keep this lift as you twist around to the left and hold the back of the chair. Work from a steady base by keeping your hips and knees level. Follow the twisting principles on page 84 to twist progressively up the spine. Stay for 10 breaths before changing sides.

Relaxing Forward Bend

Sit on the chair with your feet body-width apart. If your feet don't touch the floor easily, place a telephone book underfoot. Fold forward with a flat back to lay your ribs on your thighs. Like a rag doll, your arms just hang out of their sockets, backs of the hands on the floor, fingers softly curled. Your upper body grows heavier. Completely let go of your head and shoulders so that they release down toward the floor. Any worries drop away. Now deepen the breath, so that the front of your torso expands into the thighs and the space between them. Follow your exhalation for its entire length and observe how it lengthens effortlessly. Stay like this one to five minutes before slowly coming up.

Palming

Refresh with your own portable eyebag. Rub your hands together so the friction builds heat. Rest your elbows onto your desk and rest your head into your hands, palms over your closed eyes. Lean forward to apply a gentle pressure to your eyelids. Withdraw into yourself and observe the wave-like rhythm of your breath.

Shoulder stretches

The arm positions of Gomukhasana (see page 68) and Garudasana (see page 93) can easily be practiced in a chair and are great for office workers to ease the tensions of sitting at a desk.

EXPLORE

Your body wants to move. It was made for it! Stretch anytime using the poles at bus stops, walls or by grasping doorways to hang forward to open the chest. While watching TV, sit on floor and notice that you naturally will want to stretch when you change positions. Sit in front of the sofa and use it as a back support for squatting or Cobbler's Pose (see page 65).

Structuring Your Practice

During each session, include at least one of each type of exercise: a quiet centering exercise, a side stretch, a forward bend, a backbend, a twist, an abdominal strengthener, a balance and an inversion. Never miss the final relaxation.

Practicing in the Mornings

Your mind is quieter in the mornings. Take advantage of this mental alertness during your practice. Practice pranayama before asanas and have a period of relaxation in between. Surya Namaskar and standing poses work, warm and integrate the whole body. Backbends will enliven you and bring energy to the rest of your day.

Biralasana—Cat Pose (see page 37)

Surya Namaskar—Sun Salutation (see page 109)

Parsvakonasana— Side Angle Stretch (see page 45)

Utkatasana— Mighty Pose (see page 46)

Parsvottanasana—Chest to Leg Extension (see page 52)

Trikonasana— Triangle Pose (see page 48)

Prasarita Padottanasana— Wide Leg Stretch (see page 49)

Pavritta Trikonasana—Revolved Triangle Pose (see page 53)

Utthita Hasta Padangusthasana— Hand to Foot Pose (see page 92)

Marichyasana III –
Sage Twist III (see page 89)

Navasana –
Boat Pose (see page 95)

Bhujapidasana –
Arm Pressure Balance (see page 96)

or Bakasana –
Crane Pose (see page 97)

Paschimottanasana –
Stretch on the West Side of the Body (see page 63)

Setu Bandhasana –
Bridge Pose (see page 78)

Matsyasana –
Fish Pose (see page 79)

Urdva Dhanurasana –
Upward Facing Bow Pose (see page 80)

Another nice backbending sequence is

Salabhasana – *Locust Pose (see page 75)* **Bhujangasana –** *Cobra Pose (see page 76)* **Ustrasana –** *Camel Pose (see page 77)*

Makrasana –
Crocodile (see page 114)

Adho Mukha Svanasana –
Downward-Facing Dog (see page 100)

Sirsasana –
Headstand (see page 102)

Balasana – *Child Pose (see page 29)*

Sarvangasana –
Shoulderstand (see page 104)

Jathara Parivartanasana – *Revolved Abdominal Pose (see page 86)*

Janu Sirsasana – *Head Beyond the Knee Pose (see page 61)*

Paschimottanasana – *Stretch on the West Side of the Body (see page 63)*

Supta Konasana – *Reclined Angle Pose (see page 111)*

Balasana – *Child Pose (with knees wide) (see page 29)*

Savasana –
Corpse Pose (see page 30)

Meditation *(see page 139)*

Practicing in the Evenings

In the evenings your body is noticeably more flexible so you can extend further. On the other hand, your mind will be full of the impressions of the day and mental focus tends to be more difficult. Balance poses rein in the mind and twists help wring out any tensions from the day.

When practicing close to bedtime, allow plenty of calming poses, like forward bends, restorative poses and inversions. After yoga asanas, rest before practicing pranayama. To help you go off to sleep practice Nadi Suddhi Pranayama (see page 132). For suggested asanas for specific ailments see the section on therapeutic yoga.

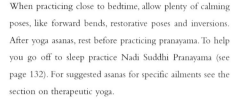

Discovering the Breath (see page 128)

Sukhasana Forward Fold— *Cross-legged Forward Fold (see page 39)*

Adho Mukha Svanasana— *Downward-Facing Dog (see page 100)*

Roll Downs (see page 38)

Trikonasana— *Triangle Pose (see page 48)*

Virabhadrasana I— *Warrior I (see page 47)*

Parsvottanasana— *Chest to Leg Extension (see page 52)*

Garudasana— *Eagle Pose (see page 93)*

Anjaneyasana— *Crescent Moon Pose (see page 74)*

Adho Mukha Svanasana— *Downward Facing Dog (see page 100)*

Uttanasana— *Intense Forward Stretch (see page 50)*

Virasana— *Hero Pose (see page 59)*

Gomukhasana— *Cow Face Pose (see page 68)*

Trianga Mukhaikapada Paschimottanasana— *Three Limbed Forward Bend (see page 60)*

Janu Sirsasana— *Head beyond the Knee Pose (see page 61)*

Ardha Baddha Padma Paschimottanasana— *Bound Half Lotus Forward Fold (see page 62)*

Pavrita Sukhasana—
Cross-Legged Twist (see page 84)

Passive Opening Out Twist
(see page 88)

Navasana—*Boat Pose*
(see page 95)

Sarvangasana—
Shoulderstand (see page 104)

or Viparita Karani - *Restorative*
Inversion (see page 113)

Halasana—*Plough Pose (see page*
106) or Salamba Halasan—
Supposrted Plough Pose (see page 115)

Karnapidasana—*Knee to Ear*
Pose (see page 107)

Passive Reclining Twist
(see page 86)

Paschimottanasana—*Stretch*
on the West Side of the Body
(see page 63)

Savasana—*Corpse Pose*
(see page 30)

Bhramari—*Humming*
Bee Breath (see page 130)

Meditation
(see page 139)

EXPLORE

*In any sequence, always include something
you really enjoy and feel good at, and do
include something that really challenges
you, so you keep extending yourself.*

Part 3

Pranayama

Pranayama

Have you ever watched children in the

playground and marvelled at their never-

ending energy? Have you ever felt that

you were more tired than you should

have been—as if the equation of energy

expenditure versus remaining energy

didn't add up?

People usually nominate food as the provider of our energy but we forget about a couple of other important sources. Ideas, for one, supply us with boundless energy. You may have experienced being so taken with an idea that you were able to work late into the night without feeling fatigued. A third energy source, recognized by yogis for millennia, is the breath.

Breath, life and energy are rooted together and yogis have a single word for all three—prana. Yogis consider death to occur when prana, the vital force, leaves the body. Conversely, when pranic levels are high, the body will be completely charged with energy. Pranayama may be translated either as restraint or control of the breath, or as pranic capacity. Pranayama exercises use breathing techniques to increase vitality and mental focus, and also as a means of expanding consciousness.

Now become aware of your breath. Maintain this awareness until you have finished reading this introduction.

We don't have to think to breathe; it is instinctive and happens automatically. The breath is usually under the control of the medulla oblongata in the relatively primitive brain stem. During pranayama breathing it shifts from being an involuntary and automatic process toward being more of a voluntary one, and it seems this activates the cerebral cortex, a more evolved part of the brain. Pranayama, by bringing a voluntary element to this involuntary process, has profound physiological, psychological and spiritual effects.

Most simply, a breath is an intake of oxygen that gets distributed to our cells. The efficient, natural breath ensures that every cell in your body receives the energy it needs to do its job: digest, grow, heal, detoxify. Logically, a healthy body will be composed of well-nourished cells. Deep, conscious breathing which fully expands the lungs has an enormously positive impact on health and enhances all cellular processes. When we breathe better, we feel better.

When you touch a baby's belly, or a kitten's or puppy's, you can feel the whole torso moving completely freely. The chest and belly open and blossom with each breath. There is a delightful inner pulsation from expansion to consolidation, a sense of real freedom. However, as we move through the process of life, we inevitably sustain some blows. Particularly as children, we have a limited capacity to understand. In response to the impacts of life, we form shielding patterns in our bodies. At some points, in some areas, our breath ceases to be the joyfully free flow it once was, and deviates into a new protective pattern. As adults we still breathe automatically and unconsciously, but due to our reactions to life, few of us breathe optimally. Those energetic children we were watching in the playground most likely still have relatively free breathing, responsive to the natural cues of the body.

Everything we do is affected by our breathing. The breath and the mind are intrinsically related; they are two expressions of the same entity. Think of the last time you felt angry or fearful: your breath became fast, shallow and irregular. Compare this to when you were dozing in a comfortable chair. Probably your breath was deeper and slower. Just as your mind affects the breath, your breath affects the mind. Yogis have long recognized that when the breath becomes calm, the mind will too. The *Hatha Yoga Pradipika*, an ancient text, tells us, "Respiration being disturbed, the mind becomes disturbed. By restraining respiration (pranayama) the Yogi attains steadiness of the mind."

The breath is a bridge to our nervous system, and enhanced breathing can improve our mental and emotional states. Firstly, by simply observing our breathing we gain a mental point of focus that can quiet the constant chatter of the mind. Secondly, it relaxes the mind to promote clear, steady thinking, decrease emotional fluctuations and provide a sense of well-being. It is a valuable tool for self-management.

Thirdly, like meditation, pranayama draws the senses inward, deepens awareness and expands consciousness.

Conscious breathing encourages conscious action and conscious living in a calmer way. For returning to the self, we have been given the miracle of the breath. A good breathing habit is a wonderful ally in life, a valuable tool for self-management when dealing with confrontations, fear, agitation, anger and confusion.

Conscious breathing is certainly a mental challenge. Did you remember to be aware of your breath just now, even as you were sitting reading?

About Practicing

The exercises fall into two categories. During exercises in returning to the natural breath (see pages 36 and 128) you immerse yourself in your true breath and begin to disentangle it from any other superimposed breathing patterns. These exercises, where you don't add anything to your breath, are a great starting place. Release any pressure you may feel to breathe "correctly" and let your instincts take over. You can repeat them every day for weeks or months to get to know your breath, and return to them as often as you wish. The remaining exercises are pranayama, some of which lead on to more advanced practices involving alteration of the breath. If you wish to develop these practices further, the best way is to work alongside an experienced teacher.

Breath awareness and pranayama are fundamental. Ideally, they should be practiced daily. Just a few minutes will still be worthwhile. Use Savasana relaxation (see page 30) to separate pranayama and asana practice so that your energies settle.

Very deep inhalations should not be practiced if you have hypertension or heart problems. Extremely long exhalations are not advisable if you suffer from low blood pressure or depression.

About
Breathing

Increase the depth of your next inhalation by about 30 percent and observe what happens to your shoulders. If you find that your shoulders lift more than a little, you are probably breathing less efficiently than you could.

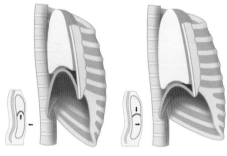

Breathing In　　　　**Breathing Out**

The shoulders lift due to the actions of the muscles around the neck and collarbone. In helping us breathe, they act as accessory muscles only. Overusing them is not an efficient way to get energy from air, so shoulder movement should account for a relatively small percentage of the effort used to inhale.

The most important muscles for breathing are those of the abdominal wall, the little muscles between the ribs, and the diaphragm. The diaphragm, being an internal muscle and harder to access, is less well understood. Like a trampoline, it spans the width of the mid-torso, separating the chest and abdominal cavities. When this large muscle is relaxed, it curves upward like an upside-down soup bowl. Every time you inhale, it contracts, and the concavity changes as this dome-shaped muscle moves downward. This downward movement increases the space in the chest cavity,

which creates a vacuum so that the spongy tissue of the lungs can draw in air from outside.

When you exhale, the diaphragm releases its contraction and moves up, reducing the size of the chest cavity and letting the air flow out of the lungs. The downward movement of the diaphragm (inhalation) increases pressure on the organs in the abdominal cavity. The upward movement (exhalation) releases the pressure. This increase and release of pressure directly affects the health of the abdominal organs. As the diaphragm moves between its downward contraction and upward relaxation, the organs are gently moved and massaged. The rhythm of the breath and free movement of the diaphragm encourage the natural pulsation that healthy organs require. To attune yourself to the movement of the diaphragm linked to the breath, practice breathing deeply in Crocodile Pose (see page 114).

How to Sit

Our bodies are as individual as our personalities, so no single position reigns supreme for pranayama or meditation. There are really only two rules for sitting. The first is to sit erect so that your head, neck and back are in line. The second is to be perfectly comfortable. Any physical discomfort will interfere with your concentration, alter your breath and undo a little of your good work.

One of the things that make pranayama special is that everyone can do it. If you can breathe, you can practice yoga! If you are ill or weak, lie down. You could use the breathing (see page 32) or, alternatively, let the torso soften down by lying flat and placing a bolster under your knees. Better still, keep yourself from drifting off to sleep by bending your knees, placing your feet on the floor a little wider than your hips, and letting the knees lean in together. If you find yourself getting sleepy, separate the knees.

Sukhasana—*Comfortable Pose*
Before practicing the cross-legged postures, use the leg cradling warm up (see page 62) to unwind the leg at the hip socket. For Sukhasana, sit cross-legged and slide your feet apart so that each foot comes to rest underneath the opposite knee. It is difficult to sit upright with your shoulders over your hips if your knees are much higher than your hips. Use cushions or folded blankets to raise your seat if necessary.

Siddhasana—*Perfect Pose*
Sit on a cushioned surface. Fold one leg in so the heel touches to the perineum—the area between the anus and the genitals. Bend the second leg and bring the heel of that foot level with the first one. Rest the backs of your hands on your knees.

Vajarasana—*Firm Pose*
Kneel with your knees and ankles together and sit down on your heels. As you bring your weight down, your inner ankles will tend to splay apart. Keep them as close together as possible. If it causes discomfort for the tops of the feet, place a small rolled blanket under them. If you like, you can place a folded blanket over your heels before sitting down.

Sitting in a Chair
Sit a little away from the backrest so your spine will be straight. If your feet don't easily touch the ground, rest them on a rolled blanket or telephone book. Fold a blanket several times to make a long pad. Experiment with it lying across the knees in any of these poses. By placing the backs of your hands on the support, your elbows will bend more and softness will come into the palms.

127

Discovering the Breath—*Breathing in All Directions*

This exercise is usually done with a partner, but can also be done alone. In position 1, lightly place your own hands where the partner's hands would be. In position 2, let your shoulders slide up and elbows fall down towards the floor as you curl your palms around your sides. Alternatively you can hug yourself, placing your hands below your armpits. In position 3, let your elbows and shoulders be as heavy and relaxed as possible as you place your hands on your back ribs. Helpers can direct their breath to the same areas as their partner. You may find that you both begin to breathe in time.

Breathing into the Front

1 Lie on your back with your knees bent and feet flat on the floor. With feet wider than hips, lean your knees together. Helpers need to be sitting perfectly comfortably so they can hold the position for the duration. Any tension will spill over to their partner. Your helper places one palm over your navel and the other high up on the chest, thumb just below the notch at the base of the throat, using a light touch to increase awareness. When you are comfortable, have your partner read the instructions to you with generous pauses after each sentence to allow you to explore.

2 Close your eyes. Observe how your body moves with each inhalation. Which part of your body moves first? Can you feel where the breath originates? What happens next? Observe the sequence of movement. What happens to the lower and upper abdomen? How does the rib cage alter? And the chest?

Which part feels like it expands more? Let the breath move you. What happens to the shoulders, the throat? Is there any tightness or constriction there? What about the face and nostrils?

3 Now turn your attention to the out breath. From where does your exhalation begin? Where does your exhalation end? Are the movements in the torso as clearly demarcated as in your inhalation? There is a yielding quality to the exhalation, a slow release as the body softens down into the floor. Can you feel a sort of consolidation in toward the center of your torso as you exhale? Could it be that the exhalation ends prematurely? Can you extend the exhalation by being patient and not rushing on to the next breath?

Breathing into the Sides

1 Maintain the quiet stillness as your partner changes position to hold the side ribs, cupping just under the armpits. Observe the horizontal expansion of the ribs on the inhalation; the outward and upward movement each time you draw air in. If you don't feel much movement, exhale more fully so that the inhalation naturally deepens. Observe how each exhalation brings a downward and inward movement.

2 Now pay attention to the timing of these movements in relation to your abdomen and chest. As you inhale, you might find the abdomen expands first, then the side ribs move up and out, and finally the upper chest expands. If this movement is difficult to isolate, then you should momentarily try to deepen your breathing so that you can discover your particular breathing pattern. What is your pattern of breathing out? Can you isolate the order of the movement of the abdomen, side ribs and chest or do they all seem to run together?

Breathing into the Back

1 Keeping your mental focus, kneel and fold forward into Child Pose. You need to be completely comfortable, so for modifications of the posture, see page 29. Your partner places their hands just below your shoulder blades, fingers wrapping around the sides.

2 Take your breath to the back of your body. Mentally direct the air into your partner's hands. As if you had little balloons under your partner's hands, feel your inhalation "puff" out against them. Have patience as you wait for the movement to come. Many people find this rather difficult and you may find that developing this awareness may take several practices.

3 In the beginning, you might find it helpful to limit your breathing into the front of the torso by slightly holding in the part of the abdomen below the navel. Visualize the breath moving into the back of the body. As well, have your partner press in slightly during your exhalation to remind you where to expand out to on the inhalation. Once you begin to get a feeling for it, feel the whole back come alive. It opens and blossoms with each inhalation, before softening down on each exhalation.

EXPLORE

Once you are able to isolate breathing into the back, you can take the breath up the spine. Each time you inhale, visualize the inhalation starting at the base of the spine and moving all the way up toward the head. Each inhalation energizes the spine, and each exhalation consolidates that energy, filling the body with prana.

Bhramari—*Humming Bee Breath*

Making sounds is a great way to bring constancy to the breath. It also lengthens the exhalation, which will naturally deepen the inhalation and encourage a slow, rhythmic breath. Don't be shy of making a sound out loud. The sound provides a point of focus for the mind. As the *Hatha Yoga Pradipika* states, "By this practice one becomes lord of the yogis and the mind is absorbed in bliss." Lose yourself in the vibrations and simply enjoy the soothing effect of Bhramari on the mind.

3

1 Sit comfortably erect or lie with your knees bent up. Have your mouth closed, jaw relaxed and the teeth slightly apart. Pressing your tongue lightly to the roof of the mouth will create a slight tension and turn the simple humming more into a bee-like droning.

2 Inhale fully, then exhale while making a humming sound. The vocal cords keep just a small amount of tension so the pitch is low. The constancy of the exhalation keeps the sound uniform. The vibration comes from the soft palate at the top of the back of the mouth. Widen the inside of the mouth to increase the resonance in the nasal cavity. Hone your awareness of the vibration to expand it out to the throat, to the top of the head, and eventually the rest of the body. Practice Bhramari for two minutes and build to five. Afterward, sit or lie quietly with eyes closed to enjoy the after-effects. Should you experience dizziness or tingling or should your mind become agitated, switch to simple breathing.

3 Another position for practice is sitting on a blanket with your knees bent up in front of you. Place your elbows on your knees so you can easily cover your eyes with your hands and the flap over your ear holes with your thumbs. Become absorbed in the sound that seems to fill the skull.

EXPLORE

Don't let stress creep in during any breathing exercise. Trying
"too hard" changes the lungs, diaphragm and nervous system,
which in turn will adversely affect your body and mind.
Evenness in the breath will lead to evenness of temperament.

Ujjayi Pranayama—*Victorious Breath*

Uj comes from the word for "up" and jaya means "triumph" or "conquest". Become victorious over any imbalance in the upward-moving prana with Ujjayi breathing. As you grow comfortable with Ujjayi breathing, use if for the duration of your asana practice.

Ujjayi breathing is a little like drinking air through a straw. The glottis lies just behind the larynx, near the male Adam's apple. It's the part of the throat that closes when you gargle or hold your breath. As the air flows past the partially closed glottis, friction is produced. This friction increases heat in the body, allowing it to stretch more than it otherwise would during yoga asana practice. Ujjayi breathing thins the breath, giving control over the flow of air into the lungs so that the breath becomes steadier, deeper and longer. More oxygen is made available, enhancing the purification and nourishment of each and every cell.

1 Sit in your meditative position. Breathe in through the nose and out through the mouth. Each time you exhale, make a long "haaaa" sound through your mouth, as if you were trying to fog up a mirror.

2 After several cycles, close your mouth midway through an exhalation, but continue to make the "haaaa" with your lips together. It will become a soft sound like a "hm" that you can feel vibrating in the back of the throat. To check if you've got it, cover your ears with your palms and listen to the internal throaty exhalation sound. It will sound like the swish of the ocean.

3 Now bring it into the inhalation. Open your mouth again and make this "haaaa" sound as you suck in the air. Close your mouth midway through to experience the soft, throaty friction again. When you feel you have got it, cover your ears to check the ocean-like quality of the sound.

4 Now you are ready for the continuous internal 'hm' breathing with your mouth closed. At first, practice Ujjayi for 10 to 20 breaths while sitting. Take breaks to return to your natural breath whenever you need. This breath is soft in nature and volume. The sound provides a point of focus for your internalized awareness. It's not necessary to breathe loudly or aggressively. While the sound produced is audible to someone close by, it's not necessary to fill the whole room. Measure the quality of your Ujjayi breathing, not by volume, but by length and steadiness. Bring your awareness to the constancy that this breath gives you. There should be no surges in the breath. It should be clean, even and pleasant. Each inhalation extends in a long, fluid way to completely fill the lungs. Likewise, the flow of air through your nostrils is slow and steady for the entire duration of the exhalation.

EXPLORE

A few rounds of Ujjayi will center you whenever you like. You can practice it whenever you are tense, or while out walking. Using Ujjayi breathing during your yoga asana practice will focus your mind. At first, discomfort in poses and other distractions will compete with the breath for your attention. In time, as you refine your breath, your pose too will refine.

Nadi Suddhi Pranayama—*Alternate Nostril Breathing*

This exercise acts as a purification (suddhi) of the subtle energy meridians (the nadis). As it helps balance the nervous system, it is useful when you feel uptight or confused. It calms the mind yet leaves you mentally alert. Practice after a hard day at work, when you feel fearful or before bed to quiet the mind for sleep.

1 Sit comfortably. Curl the index and middle fingers of your right hand into the palm. Inhale fully through both nostrils.

2 Close the right nostril with the thumb of the right hand and exhale fully through the left nostril.

3 Still keeping the right thumb covering the right nostril, now inhale through the left side.

4 Close the left nostril with your ring and little finger.

5 Release your thumb and exhale through the right nostril.

6 Inhale through the right side.

7 Close the right nostril and exhale through the left.

This is one cycle. Complete three to seven cycles before resting your arm down, and breathing quietly through both nostrils. Wait until you feel ready before starting the next round. Complete three to seven rounds and finish by relaxing in Savasana (see page 30).

The air moves through the nostrils at a constant rate. From beginning to end, during each inhalation and exhalation, the air flows at the same speed. There is no strain and the breath will have a soft quality. Visualize a saucer of fine wood ash just under your nose. If you inhale too greedily the ash would be sucked inside your nose. If you exhale forcefully, it would end up settling over your clothes.

During the practice, keep your right elbow raised to avoid placing pressure on your chest and impeding the lungs from filling. Tension can build up in the shoulder and arm so change hands as necessary. Open your eyes occasionally to check that your head is straight, not tilted off to one side.

Nostril Dominance

You might notice that one nostril feels more open than the other. Each nostril relates to an energy channel (nadi) which, according to esoteric anatomy, runs up the side of the vertebral column. The right nostril corresponds to the Pingala Nadi, which is more intellectually alert, aware, active; a more "masculine" energy similar to the yang of Chinese medicine. It is the perfect one to have open during an exam as it relates to intellectual pursuits, rational thought, attention to detail, vigorous physical action and digesting food. The left nostril relates to the Ida Nadi and

3

emotions and fatigue. If you are having trouble falling asleep, check if the right nostril is dominant and switch to the left. To change nostril dominance, lie on the side opposite to the nostril you would like to open. A vigorous walk will open the right nostril.

4

5

corresponds to the "feminine" (yin) traits of intuition, creative processes, holistic and imaginative thinking. It would be a good nostril to have open when you need to make a subjective decision, play music, or when you need slow, sustained energy expenditure. Nadi Suddhi pranayama helps balance these two important pranic pathways. To test which nadi is more active at any time, place the back of the hand under the nose and exhale.

Dominance changes at about 30- to 120-minute intervals throughout the day. Nostril dominance is affected by eating,

EXPLORE

Once your Nadi Suddhi practice develops, implement a count so that the inhalations and exhalations are of equal length. Choose a number or beats that is in no way stressful to keep up. Over weeks, increase the count. It should always feel flowing and natural, never strained. Force is counterproductive in pranayama so if you find yourself tensing, then reduce the count.

Part 4

Meditation

Meditation

Gazing at the sun with wide-open eyes

blinds the vision. If you don't stare at it

directly, but instead look away a little, you

can get a sense of it. Meditation is like

that. A change of focus reduces the glare

of superfluous distractions and helps us

see past the false perceptions to contact

the peace and happiness that reside within.

Meditation quietens the mind. Of the eight limbs of yoga, it is placed seventh, close to the culmination of the state of Yoga—the cessation of all the fluctuations of the thoughts. During meditation, we open up the space between the end of one thought and the beginning of the new one.

Meditators do not tune out life's challenges. Rather, they gain greater insight into their perceptions and their response to stressful situations. As the brain patterns merge into the theta state—deeper than sleep—the meditator experiences a state of restful alertness; fully conscious and aware. In meditation we practice being the observer, not the doer. We observe our thoughts and remain detached, without altering the thought patterns at all. Remaining neutral toward our thoughts means that we do not lend them energy to disturb the mind. Whereas before you might have been seeing

yourself and the world in a dusty mirror, meditation helps to wipe the mirror clean, for new perceptions and reflections.

Studies—Blood pressure

Many studies have been done on meditation, particularly Transcendental Meditation (TM), which involves meditation using a mantra for 20 minutes, twice a day. A study was made in 1996 on hypertensive African-Americans in California. It found that TM significantly lowered blood pressure—more than did any other relaxation technique or education and lifestyle changes. Those who practiced TM for three months saw an average reduction of 10 to 12 points in systolic blood pressure and six to eight points in diastolic pressure (similar results to those of antihypertensive drugs). Through meditation, participants had decreased their risk of heart attack by 11 percent, and stroke by 8-15 percent.

Stress and Related diseases

Researchers at Harvard Medical School used MRI technology to monitor brain activity on meditators. They found that meditation activates the sections of the brain in charge of the autonomic nervous system. This governs the functions in our bodies that we can't control, such as digestion and blood pressure. As these functions are often compromised by stress, it could mean that, by lessening the adrenaline surges usually made as a response to stress, meditation would help to decrease stress-related conditions such as hypertension, heart disease, asthma, insomnia, digestive problems and so on.

A study on stress levels was published in the American Journal of Health Promotion. Sixty-two people who reported abnormally high levels of stress participated. Twenty-seven people were the control group. Thirty-five underwent 28 hours of "mindfulness training" involving meditation, yoga postures and stress-relief techniques over two months. By the end of three months, the mindfulness trainees reported a 54 percent drop in psychological distress, as well as a 46 percent reduction in medical symptoms. The control group reported no improvement in psychological symptoms and a slight increase in medical complaints.

Healing

The word meditation comes from the Latin root meditor, which literally means "healing", and meditation has been found to reduce costs in health care. In Canada, researchers tracked a group of 677 people enrolled in a health insurance program. After learning TM, their health care payments were reduced by 5-7 percent cumulatively every year. After seven years, health costs had been cut by almost 50 percent. Another study of health insurance statistics was published in Psychosomatic Medicine. It studied more than 2,000 people practicing TM over a five-year period. It found they had 50 percent fewer doctors' visits and fewer than half the hospitalizations than other groups of similar age, profession and insurance coverage. Meditators had fewer incidents of illness in 17 categories, including 87 percent fewer hospitalizations for heart disease and 55 percent fewer for cancer.

Intelligence

A study published in the British journal *Personal and Individual Differences* showed that students practicing transcendental meditation increased their IQ by five points in two years and by nine points in four years.

Ageing

Meditation has even been found to slow ageing. A study in *The International Journal of Neuroscience* found that a group of 50-year-olds who had been practicing transcendental meditation for over five years showed a 12-year decrease in "biological age" as compared to controls. And in the words of one old timer, "Meditators grow older but they don't necessarily have to grow old".

An ancient healer stated "Man is ill, because he is never still." In India, teachers often refer to our monkey-like minds, which flit around randomly. The Vedas, the earliest known compilations of Indian spiritual writings, say the mind is harder to control than the wind. Achieving the cessation of thought patterns is certainly a tall order. But don't be disheartened. Even if you never arrive at this point, enormous benefits can be derived along the path. The Latin root word *meditor* comes from the Sanskrit *madha*, meaning wisdom. Meditators feel that meditation improves their quality of life and gives them a sense of the inner peace that is at the core of all of us. This super-conscious state allows us to re-center. We tap into a positive universal energy, something greater than ourselves. It gives a wonderful feeling of being completely known—sort of like the feeling you have when your beloved has seen all of you, good and bad, and still loves you. Meditation is a source of great inner strength and is something wonderful to come home to.

Yogamudrasana—*Sealing Pose*

This pose quietens the mind and is a good preparation pose for meditation. Alternatively, you can practice becoming absorbed in the breath (see page 128), Bhramari (see page 130) or several rounds of Nadi Suddhi Pranayama (see page 132).

Sit in Siddhasana (see page 127) by first folding your right leg in, then bringing the left heel in front of the right. Grasp your left wrist with your right hand behind your back. Inhale and extend the torso upward, then exhale and fold forward bringing your forehead to the floor. Rest like this for at least a minute, observing the breath and the mind. Then, with the eyes closed, come up to sitting and change sides with the legs and hands before repeating.

For the mind to quieten you need to be physically comfortable. If this seated position does not feel steady and easy, then practice while sitting on the heels. Rest the forehead on a folded blanket if necessary.

About Mudras

Whereas bandhas (see page 15) are powerful energy locks, mudras, or energy seals, act more gently. Yogis believe that mudras stimulate the flow of prana through the body and seal it in so it's not lost. Some mudras are similar to asanas. Others are hand gestures that may be used during pranayama or meditation. A number of mudras are linked with the chakras. If a mudra also involves contraction of the muscles, then it becomes a bandha.

Useful Mudras for Meditation

Mudras influence the subtle bodies and increase receptiveness to higher states of consciousness.

For **Gyana Mudra** (also called Jnana Mudra) join the tip of the thumb and index fingers while keeping the other fingers straight.

For **Bhajrava Mudra** (Gesture of Shiva) place your right hand on your left. Rest your hands in your lap, with your palms facing up and let the tips of your thumbs touch.

How to Meditate

1 Set the Body

A natural time for meditation is at the end of your yoga asana practice, when the body is warm and loose. Otherwise, before beginning to meditate do a few limbering stretches that release your body and bring you into the present moment. You can practice Yogamudrasana (see page 138), Discovering the Breath (see page 128), Bhramari breathing (see page 130) or several rounds of Nadi Suddhi Pranayama (see page 132).

2 Set the Mind

First decide how long you will sit for. Choose a quiet place to meditate and turn off the phone. Cover yourself with a blanket or shawl if necessary. Assume your meditative position, making sure the back, neck and head are in line. See the pranayama section (page 127) for suggested sitting positions.

Some people like to offer a personal prayer or chant as a little ritual to carry them into the session. In any case, whether you do this or not, clarify your intention, reminding yourself of your higher goal and your reason for meditating.

3 Relax the Body

While seated, mentally check in with each part of the body. Start from your toes and relax everything bit by bit up to the crown of your head. Once relaxed, commit to not moving your body any more. Any physical movement only serves to distract.

4 Focus the Mind

The breath is a wonderful tool to deepen concentration. Begin by observing the flow of air through the nostrils. Observe the minute sensations at the nostrils: the cool air as it flows in through the nostrils, and the warmed air that flows out. There is no need to judge your breath or change the way you are breathing. Patiently be aware simply of what is. You are the detached observer. Practicing detachment in this way is useful for the times in life that you are challenged by pain or difficulty. If you like, count your breaths in rounds of ten.

5 Expansion of Consciousness

Steer your thoughts to an attitudinal theme or virtue; a hyper-goal such as freedom from attachments, inner peace or spiritual self-realization.

6 Finally

To close, repeat a prayer or use a chant if you find it helpful. When your time for sitting has ended, don't jump up and start racing through your day in an automated way. You have just connected with your inner self with a greater force. Stay mindful and carry this sensation through into your daily life and personal relationships.

Meditation Techniques

Meditation is a deeply personal thing. More than a technique or a practice, meditation is an experience. There is no one way that is better than another. Try out some ways to see what you feel works best for you. After some experimentation, find a technique with which you feel an affinity and stick to it for at least several months.

Chakra Meditation

By moving your awareness to the appropriate physical spot on the body you can meditate on a chakra. Each chakra has a seed sound associated with it that you can use as a mantra. Alternatively, you may choose to meditate on the pure color of the chakra (see page 147 for chakra mantras and colors).

Trataka—Steady Gazing

Trataka is a good practice for dharana, or concentration, the sixth limb of yoga. You may gaze at a lit candle, picture, symbol or deity to which you feel drawn. Over time, trataka moves from being a concentration exercise to become a meditation.

Moving Meditation

Any action performed with mindfulness can be meditative. A walking meditation is useful if you find sitting for long periods very uncomfortable, or if you tend to fall asleep. You might begin sitting, then, when you are ready, stand up. Keep your eyes unfocused, gazing down to the floor. Walk with your awareness on the feet. Feel the sensations in each sole as it rolls down to contact the floor, bears weight, and then peels off the floor to take the next step. Stay keenly focused on the changes in the weight borne by each foot as you slowly walk in a circle. After this walking meditation, sit and continue the meditation.

Mantra Meditation

Many people derive great benefit from using a mantra. See the next section on page 142 for more information on mantras.

Themed Meditations

Choose a subject on which you would like to expand your awareness, such as love or peace. During breath or mantra meditation you attempt to confine the thoughts to a single subject—the breath or the mantra. In a themed meditation you can expand your consciousness by further refining the focus: from many thoughts around a subject, you can reduce down to a single thought on it.

The aim is not to prevent all thought but to attain a one-pointed awareness. Observe the flow of thought, like ripples in a lake, without following them. If you follow a thought that isn't the focus of your meditation, you are lending it the energy to distract yourself. Practice mastery over the mind and gently bring your mind back to your chosen subject. The constant churning of the mind eventually gives way to peacefulness.

Right: The aim of meditation is not to prevent all thought but to attain a one-pointed awareness.

More on Meditation

Set aside a regular time to meditate. Yogis believe the best times of day to meditate are sunrise, noon, sunset or midnight, but the most important thing is to find a time in your schedule that you know you will be able to stick to. Don't set yourself up for failure by choosing an impossible time. Likewise, decide realistically for how long you can dedicate to each meditation. Then keep to it—don't come out of it early. Some people use a timer set to beep gently when the time has elapsed.

Traditionally, east- or north-facing positions are considered conducive to spiritual practice.

Sitting perfectly still can become difficult as every physical sensation is magnified. Breathe through itches as they arise. Remind yourself that all things change; these sensations are only transitory, and can provide the energy for better focus. For a busy mind, being mindful—doing nothing except paying attention—gets boring. Instead of inventing things to relieve this boredom, stay with the meditation, accept that you are feeling bored, and make it the subject of your attention for a while.

Although meditation brings people peace, it can also bring to mind other issues. As a process of self-observation, you may be confronted with thoughts or parts of your character that you would prefer not to recognize. Facing certain feelings you are not owning up to can raise your level of anxiety, as if there is nowhere to hide. Although it can be very disturbing, remind yourself that all things change. Becoming aware of your shadow side actually allows you to operate in a different way.

Like your yoga practice, meditation experiences will vary from day to day. Don't classify meditations as "good" or "bad". Perhaps a meditation feels "bad" because it has thrown up something you find uncomfortable. This might make it feel more difficult but could also actually offer you a lot. Try not to become too attached to the highs you experience on your spiritual path either. If we cling to these feelings we may miss the point of the exercise, which is to have a feeling of unity with the universe as a whole. Refrain from judging the highs and lows and simply welcome that experience as part of the unceasing flow of life.

In meditation, we often seek to encourage a detachment from worldly things. While this type of detachment can assist us in objective observation, it does not mean that we should stop caring about what happens to the world. We need to continue interacting in an open-minded and loving way.

Mantras and Chanting

A mantra is a potent sound that helps harmonize the system, a vibrational force that carries healing. Reciting a mantra or devotional verse in a yogic chant is uplifting and soothing.

Mantra

A mantra can be a syllable, a single word or a phrase that is generally repeated over and over. Using a mantra provides a point of focus for the mind. A mantra acts as a positive affirmation; a constant reminder, and a way to bring yourself back to your base. Reciting a mantra is an exercise in dharana (concentration) that can become dhyana (meditation).

Many mantras are in the ancient language of Sanskrit. Sanskrit is made up of primordial sounds and each syllable creates a particular resonance within the body. A Sanskrit mantra is a particular combination of sound vibrations that, when chanted or meditated upon, has a specific effect on the body, mind and psyche. This resonance assists healing and spiritual elevation. In each repetition a certain energetic vibration is being sent out into the world. For this reason the pronunciation needs to be correct, so if you are not sure, ask a yoga teacher about the correct pronunciation for your mantra.

Though traditionally given by a guru, you can certainly choose your own mantra. It is not necessary to have an exotic-sounding mantra. You may feel more affinity with a mantra in your own language such as *peace*, *love* or *faith*.

If you would like to use a mantra for meditation, you can begin each session by chanting the mantra aloud and letting the resonance flow through the body. Then, keeping the reverberation, take the volume down to a whisper, and, finally, continue your meditation by repeating it mentally.

Mantra is often used as a way of focussing at the beginning and end of a yoga class. It can be as simple as chanting *om* three times with the teacher. You can link your mantra practice to work with particular areas of the body and the chakras (see page 146). Many people find using a mantra helps them in times of stress—even in public places a mantra can be repeated silently. Like an affirmation, it acts as a helpful reminder to bring you back to base.

Some Common Mantras

Om—This sacred syllable is considered the mother of all sounds. As with other Sanskrit mantras, it is believed that it sets up a special vibration in your body and mind, and this is spread out into the world. It is used by both Hindus and Buddhists. Om is composed of the three sounds A-U-Mmmm running together. The first "A" sound will resonate more in the belly. The "U" moves the vibration up to the chest cavity. The final long "M" sound is made into a nasal sound so its resonance is felt more in the head.

Om namah shivaya—This is a salutation to the Hindu deity Shiva. Non-Hindus use this mantra too, intending it to honour the divine in oneself.

Soham—This mantra also honours the divine within. Pronounced so-hum, it means "I am the universal self".

Shanti—Means "peace" in Sanskrit.

Om namo bhagavate vasudevaya—Means salutations to the Divine Source, the indweller of all.

Chanting

Though some adults feel shy about making sounds out loud, chanting is really perfectly natural. Let go of worrying about how good or bad you sound. Chanting is not like singing but more like reciting. The purpose is not to have the most beautiful voice, but rather to feel the sound resonate through the body.

The devotional path of yoga is called Bhakti Yoga where God or God's representative spiritual teacher is worshipped. In Bhakti Yoga, spiritual verses are chanted with fervent devotion. This brings a sense of connection to something greater than the self, the universal consciousness, as the heart center opens up to a crescendo of universal love. Then the emotions are settled down to stabilize once more. This climax and settling of the emotions is similar to a heart-broken person crying out a song about lost love. When the emotions are relived in a small way, then left to settle, it's very healing on the emotional sphere.

Even if you don't consider yourself religious, chanting can be a worthwhile and fulfilling experience. A chanting session is incredibly soothing. It feels like a balm for the brain. It seems to wipe away all the usual preoccupations, so chanting is like taking an instant mental holiday. In addition, it clarifies your intentions and is uplifting for the heart. If you are not comfortable with a chant to God, you may feel more comfortable interpreting it as being a chant to the light you carry within. If you ask around, you may find a chanting group in your area that you can join.

Chants to Start and Finish Your Yoga Practice

Om asathoma sadgamaya
Thamasoma Jyotirgamaya
Mrithyorma Amrithangamaya
Om Shanti Shanti Shanti

Om Lead me from the unreal to the real
From darkness to light
From the predicament of death to immortality
Om peace, peace, peace

Om
Swasthi praja bhyah pari pala yantam
Nya yena margena mahi mahi shaha
Go brahmanebhyaha shubhamastu nityam
Lokaa samastha sukhino bhavantu
Om

Om
Let prosperity be glorified
Let rulers rule the world with law and justice
Let divinity and wisdom be protected
Let people of the world be happy and prosperous
Om

Part 5

The Kundalini Path

Chakras

Hatha yoga exercises focus on the
vertebral column and work not only
on the physical body but also on the
subtle bodies. The twisting, lengthening
and bending forward, backward and
sideways of Hatha Yoga aim to awaken
and balance the subtle energies.

According to the yogic tradition, there are many thousands of nadis—energy meridians—in our bodies. The largest one is called the Sushumna Nadi. It is not recognized by Western anatomy but it follows a nervous pathway, running from the perineum up the length of the vertebral column.

Yogis speak of a reservoir of energy known as the kundalini, which resides in the body. Literally translated as "she who is coiled", the kundalini force is likened to a serpent lying dormant at the base of the spine. Yoga exercises seek to clear the energy path by undoing any energy blockages of the spine, and purify the body and mind to clear the way for this cosmic power to rise. Another way to clear the kundalini path is to work with the chakras.

The word chakra means "wheel" in Sanskrit. A chakra, like a wheel or vortex, is an area of increased energy (prana).

As a center of energy, a chakra can exist anywhere in the body, though we tend to recognize seven main ones located at various levels up the spine. It is said that the chakras act as transformers. Since each chakra has a related nerve and endocrine plexus, they are believed to channel the pranic energy into the physical body at the points of the chakras. It is thought that when all the chakras are fully functioning, the kundalini power can move unimpeded up the body's central energy channel from the base of the spine to the crown of the head. As the kundalini "serpent" uncoils and rises, it enlivens each chakra in turn. When it reaches the top chakra, it is said that a change of consciousness occurs, special psychic powers are obtained and liberation of the soul (the ultimate goal of yoga) is attained.

Each of these seven reservoirs of energy has its own physical, emotional and spiritual effects. The lower chakras from the base of the spine to the solar plexus are considered to be more physical than the chakras located from the heart to the crown of the head. Many people choose to focus their work on the higher chakras, believing them to be more 'spiritual' than the more earthy lower ones. However, like building a house, each level needs to be supported by a solid base below it. The grounding forces of the lower chakras provide the vital and steady foundation for balanced spiritual exploration. Should a chakra be out of balance, yoga can help stimulate the less active chakras and move energy along from areas where it is congested, thereby balancing the whole system. Knowledge of the chakras is a means of understanding ourselves a little more; yoga postures are the tools with which to facilitate transformation.

1 Muladhara Chakra—*Root Chakra*

Location

The base of the spine is the home of the first chakra, known as the root chakra. The related organs are the organs of elimination and excretion—the lungs, skin, kidneys, large intestine and rectum.

Expression

The root chakra governs your connection to the earth and how "rooted" you feel. It deals with your material and monetary existence. It is the chakra that is concerned with getting your basic needs met—needs such as obtaining food, shelter and even love. It is very involved with how stable you feel both emotionally and in your physical set-up. The root chakra is expressed in your strength and stamina. It gives you the drive to get up and go to work in the morning. It allows you to focus, be disciplined, stay healthy and also to be aware of your limits.

The root chakra must be balanced as a foundation to balancing the other chakras or your progression will be without roots and stability. When the muladhara chakra is out of balance, it may cause problems of the lower abdominal area such as constipation, diarrhoea, haemorrhoids, kidney problems, sciatica and back pain.

Since the base chakra has such a grounding force, the psychological impact of imbalance at the level of this chakra can swing from being too grounded to not being grounded enough. A lack of grounding could cause you to live in a fantasy world and feel off-center. You could experience difficulty focusing, or find you go out of control easily.

Chakras at a Glance

	Chakra	Color	Element	Relates to	Element	Mantra
	Muladhara	Red	Ruby	Stability, Survival, Basic Needs	Earth	Lam
	Svadhisthana	Orange	Amber	Creativity, Sexuality, Relationships	Water	Vam
	Manipura	Yellow	Gold	Power, Will, Action	Fire	Ram
	Anahata	Green	Emerald	Unconditional Love, Self-Healing, Joy	Air	Yam
	Visuddha	Sky Blue	Sapphire	Communication, Self-Expression, Truth	Ether	Ham
	Ajna	Indigo	Diamond	Intuition, Wisdom	Pure Essence	Om
	Sahasrara	Violet	Amethyst	Spiritual Illumination, The Bliss State	Boundlessness	(no mantra)

You may find it hard to contain your feelings. On the other hand there may be too much holding on, for example if you are excessively materialistic or unable to let go of things emotionally. It might manifest itself in being overly controlling and trying to keep a hold over others.

The muladhara chakra is the driving force behind the energy to work. When this chakra is not in balance, you could become overly attached to your work, leading to a workaholic lifestyle. Another manifestation could be diminished creative power, which will interfere with your ability to enjoy life and prevent you from opening up to feelings of joy and happiness.

Aggressiveness and stubbornness can be further signs of root chakra imbalance, as can a tendency towards selfishness, creating material and emotional possessiveness. An imbalance in the root chakra can make you self-serving and self-centered. When your survival is threatened, you feel afraid. This fear can be immobilizing and ultimately prevent you from achieving your goals. The root chakra is awakened when you confront your fears.

When the root chakra is functioning well, there will be good general health for the related organs, like the kidneys and bowel. The adrenal glands, involved in the response to stress, will be healthy, not exhausted from chronic over-stimulation. There will be a cheerful, fearless and courageous attitude. A balanced base chakra brings self-confidence, enthusiasm, a strong will to live and a clear sense of identity. Trust in others comes easily in this state.

You will have a good perspective on life and be able to stay in touch with the greater scheme of things. You will be able to detach from an over-emphasis on the importance of material possessions. There will be a healthy attitude to work. While you will remain focused, you will not be so attached to your work that you ignore other parts of your life. You will approach your work and challenges with enthusiasm and joy. With this attitude, you find that material success can come to you more easily.

2 Svadhisthana Chakra—
Sexual Chakra

Location

The second chakra is located at the lower abdomen between the navel and the genitals. The second chakra governs the organs of the lower abdominal area such as those of the urinary and reproductive systems.

Expression

Its location is a clue that the second chakra is involved with sexuality, relationships and creativity. The svadhisthana chakra governs our nurturing abilities, and our sensation and pleasure focus. It is also highly involved in relationships, and this includes your relationship with yourself.

Change is an inescapable fact of life. Without change, there is no growth, no movement, no life. The sexual chakra is connected with change and how you deal with it. A well-balanced second chakra allows you to go with the flow and alter your path as necessary.

If you have an imbalance in this chakra, it could affect the urinary, reproductive and circulatory systems. Impotence, sexually transmitted diseases and bladder problems could be signs that the second chakra needs some attention.

People who have an unbalanced sexual chakra have difficulty with giving or receiving either materially or emotionally. Physically, obesity can be a result of a lack of balance between giving and receiving. An overweight person who is consuming more calories than they are using is taking more than they are giving. The second chakra also helps with the assimilation of knowledge. On the mental level, receiving is linked with the integration of knowledge as the brain takes in and stores information.

Feelings of guilt, anxiety, unpredictability and clinging on can be an indication of an unbalanced second chakra. Some people may have difficulty separating their own feelings from those of others. General low energy or lack of creativity can also be connected to this chakra. There may be too little or too much sexual desire. Flirting outrageously or using sex to gain attention are further signs that the chakra is off balance. A person may become trapped in an unhealthy pattern of seeking excessive sensual pleasure.

A person with a well-balanced second chakra has a high level of general vitality. The lower abdominal, urinary and reproductive systems will all be healthy. If this chakra is balanced, you will be outgoing, patient and have a good sense of humor. You will be comfortable with your own sexuality and content with yourself. You will also find it easy to be positive and enjoy life.

A main force of this chakra governs the attraction of opposites. There is an unceasing dance between dualities. Movement is created and you can easily go with the flow of life. At the same time, you have intellectual ideas about the world and how your desires and emotions fit in it.

Creative problem-solving and the ability to work creatively with others will come easily. Even if other people have different ideas from you, you are able to work out a complementary path. Rather than forming obstacles, the different approaches and attitudes of others enrich your life and allow you to develop and grow.

3 Manipura Chakra—
Solar Plexus

Location

The third chakra is situated between the bottom of the breastbone and the navel. It controls the digestive system and related organs including the liver, stomach, gallbladder, pancreas, spleen and the organs of excretion.

Expression

Through its closeness to the digestive system, this third chakra is involved in the production and storage of energy— the same energy that allows us to live our lives effectively.

The manipura chakra relates to emotions, actions, power and will. It helps us recognize that, with effort and action, we can achieve what we want.

The solar plexus center links to your level of comfort with power, and this includes your sense of personal power. Your power comes through being able to bring things together. Rather than seeing things as separate and unrelated, and subdividing them, you are able to find the power in unification. A balanced third chakra helps you develop a healthy will and autonomy. When unbalanced, you may feel powerless, have lower self-esteem and be more easily swayed by the opinions of those around you.

If your third chakra is not in balance, you can experience uncontrolled extreme emotions such as violent passions, jealousies, anger and frustration, and these can then turn into troubling doubts, fears and confusion. There may also be a tendency to try to manipulate others. Obsessive characteristics or a tendency toward having an addictive personality might also appear.

Failure to learn to assert your own autonomy can cause you to feel powerless or victimised. With an unbalanced third chakra, you risk running out of emotional steam. Apathy and lethargy cause your energy to turn in on itself and make you want to withdraw from life. You can become overly critical of yourself, causing you to lose the ability to connect and be nourished by your surroundings. Low self-esteem makes you doubt yourself and as a result you can suffer self-recrimination.

There can also be an imbalance of fiery energy. This may manifest itself as feeling hot, avoiding spicy foods, wanting cold drinks, sweating easily or being quick-tempered. Too little fire, on the other hand, can cause you to feel cold, crave hot, spicy foods and hot drinks or feel slow and lethargic. Any of the related organs might show symptoms. Internally, ulcers, upset stomach, diabetes, hypoglycemia or even alcoholism, and, externally, a tight hard belly, large potbelly or a sunken diaphragm, may all indicate an imbalance.

A well-balanced manipura chakra gives a great deal of energy, which might show up as having a warm body and fast metabolism. This energy brings an enthusiasm for work, play, development and transformation in your life. You will feel bright, extroverted and clear thinking.

You will have a constructive use of power and it will be directed inward toward the self instead of being wielded over others. This internal willpower creates proactive, assertive and confident qualities. Your self-esteem is at a healthy level and there will be a drive toward a consciously controlled positive change, as opposed to passively waiting or wishing for something great to happen. You will be self-motivated and self-accepting. You will be naturally aware of your social responsibility and will approach things from a social perspective. You aren't tempted to abuse your power to manipulate others. Your power is used to bring people and things together rather than to drive them apart. A balanced manipura chakra produces an inner strength allowing you to perform actions with ease and grace.

4 Anahata Chakra—
Heart Center

Location

Located at the center of the chest, the anahata chakra corresponds to love in the pure, unconditional sense. It encompasses the love of nature and the love of all humanity.

Expression

Physically, the anahata chakra relates to the heart, the circulatory and respiratory systems, the breasts, chest and shoulders. The fourth chakra brings together the forces of the first three chakras. The first chakra is about solidity and stability, the second governs change and movement, while the third brings into play acceptance and the forces of the will. When these forces come together, they can then be transformed into energies to achieve higher goals. The heart center is the point of transition between the more grounding lower chakras and the higher, spiritual ones.

The heart chakra deals with social awareness, love and openness, a sense of devotion, peace, forgiveness, acceptance, kindness and joy. While the second chakra has a unifying force that is oriented more to objects or people, the unifying force of the heart chakra is experienced more as a state of being. It is less involved with sexuality, less materialistic and more conceptual. It deals with the union and harmonious integration of the self into larger social groups without any loss of true sense of self. The force of the anahata chakra allows us to break out of the limitations of our ego. In transcending the ego we can grow toward something deep and strong. It loosens our boundaries as we experience the joy of love.

Physically, an imbalance in the fourth chakra could result in heart conditions, including high blood pressure, and could cause respiratory conditions, asthma and arthritis of the arms. Emotionally, you might tend toward feeling a conditional type of love. Perhaps you expect something in return for giving your love, or you could confuse love and sex. You may impose your will over others, and tend to be manipulative. On the other hand, you might be overly selfless, often finding yourself in the role of martyr. An imbalance might lead to a lack of sensitivity, arrogance, selfishness or feelings of sadness or depression.

When the heart chakra is in balance the related organs and systems will be healthy. There is a sense of connection with all life, which gives peace, joy and feelings of unconditional love for all beings. Your relationships will be more balanced and harmonious. Your emotions will be free but not unstable and they can be clearly and spontaneously expressed. You will be open, willing and able to live without fear of vulnerability. There will be a good balance between the material things in life and your emotions. Because the heart center has an integrative force, helping us overcome dualities, and because love is the ultimate healing energy, the heart chakra is the center for healing.

5 Visuddha Chakra—
Throat Center

Location

Located level with the base of the throat, the fifth chakra is linked to communication and expression.

Expression

As its physical location may suggest, the visuddha chakra corresponds to the neck and organs of the neck, including the voice box and airway in the throat. As the related glands are the thyroid and parathyroid glands, the metabolism of the whole body is affected by the fifth chakra.

The throat chakra is involved in the verbal expression of all the thoughts and feelings encompassed by the lower chakras. It affects our speech and how we express ourselves. It is linked to truth and honesty. This center connects our feelings and intuition with our thoughts, making them enter our consciousness and enabling us to act on them. The throat chakra helps form our future. A need or desire is more easily met once it is expressed, so, in a way, we shape our own futures with verbal communication. Like the second chakra, this fifth chakra is strongly linked to creativity: the formation of speech, communication and expression is an inherently creative process. The throat chakra moves away from the physicality of the chakras below. Its boundaries are more fluid and less physical, being involved in such things as the sharing of information and ideas.

Problems with the throat chakra can show up physically in sore throats, loss of voice and neck or throat conditions. An over- or under-active thyroid, headaches from neck muscle tension, insomnia, flu and even cancer could be manifestations of an imbalance in this center. Any difficulty in expression or communication indicates an imbalance of the fifth chakra. You may hold back, either in voicing your opinion, or showing your thoughts or feelings. On the other hand, you may dominate conversations and discussions.

Perhaps you have difficulty expressing your needs or having them met. You could be critical, tactless, deceitful, judgmental, or harsh-voiced or may suffer from false pride.

When the throat chakra is in balance, the throat area will be physically healthy. You have effective expression and clear communication of your feelings and ideas, and it can show in your voice, making it clear and pleasant to the ear. Creativity, maturity and inspiration help you deal with yourself and others in an honest, compassionate and tactful way. You can make clear assessments without judging others. Verbal expression is made possible by vibrational rhythms, and the throat chakra is linked to rhythm and the pace at which we lead our lives. You will be able to conduct your life at a regular, easy pace rather than losing yourself in a hectic and destructive lifestyle. A balanced fifth chakra gives you a sense of serenity and devotion.

6 Ajna Chakra—
Third Eye Center

Location

Located between and just above the eyebrows, the sixth chakra is like a third eye, said to be the seat of wisdom.

Expression

The sixth chakra is linked to the brain and nervous system. The ears, nose, eyes and sinuses relate to it. Lastly, the hormonal system is affected by the sixth chakra through the wide-reaching effects of the pituitary gland in the brain. The information-gathering capability of our sense of sight is very powerful. With a single glance we can take on board an enormous amount of information. Taking our ability to 'see' and assess situations further, the sixth chakra becomes involved in the capacity for intuition, imagination, visualization and even clairvoyance. This intuition is the link between our intellectual and psychic abilities. Being guided from within lies beyond the part of the mind telling us we can't do something and the part telling us we can. Intuition is a line to a force greater than ourselves. Physically, an imbalance in the sixth chakra may manifest itself in headaches or eye, ear, nose and sinus conditions. Hormonal imbalances, insomnia and nervous disorders may appear. Depression may arise. The third eye center is linked to the hormonal glands of the brain, and therefore to levels of the neurotransmitter serotonin, which has been linked to depression.

On another level, depression might come from having lost touch with your essentially creative self—a lack of ability to use and flow with your creativity. When the sixth chakra is out of balance, you can have problems focusing and concentrating and may feel confused and negative. A lack of direction and intellectual stagnation can be experienced. So many people spend many hours a week in a job that doesn't enhance their life. We need to be enriched by what we do. Make sure your work is in harmony with your beliefs. The sixth chakra can help us determine what will enrich us. Your yoga asana practice is useful as it is a journey on the emotional and intellectual level, which opens you up to listen to your intuitive self and the special language of your body; posture, holding patterns, disease, well-being.

When the third eye chakra is in balance, you will be able to observe thoughts and feelings without becoming overly attached to them. You have a good level of direction, devotion and high ideals. You are imaginative and carry within yourself a sense of oneness, a feeling of unity. This sense of integration allows you to overcome anxiety. When the ajna chakra is fully awakened, you experience a mastery of the self, known as self-realization.

7 Sahasrara Chakra—
Crown Center

Location

The crown chakra is located at the top of the head, at the "soft spot" that is the anterior fontanel.

Expression

The brain, the whole nervous system and the pineal gland are in the realm of the crown chakra. The root chakra and the crown chakras have opposite forces. While the root chakra acts as the entry point of human life, the crown acts as an exit point. The crown chakra deals with transcending materialism and letting go of physical attachments. The search for meaning—the understanding that all things are part of a larger structure—brings us closer to unity. The seventh chakra gives us a coherent sense of meaning. It relates to the highest state of consciousness. It deals with spiritual enlightenment, self-realization and God consciousness. The crown chakra is very important as it is the point where the liberation of the soul arrives. When the sahasrara chakra is fully awakened, there is a fusion of the seven chakras and the experience of spiritual boundlessness. At this level of consciousness, there is an awareness of a higher or deeper order that integrates and unifies. It reminds us that, even though the body is finite, the soul is infinite.

Physically, cerebral tumours and increased pressure in the skull can be an indication of an imbalance in the crown center. There could be psychological symptoms like psychoses or neuroses or depression. Insomnia may occur due to the crown chakra's link with the pineal gland, which produces melatonin, vital for healthy sleep and is linked to Seasonal Affective Disorder Syndrome (SADS), sufferers of which feel down and depressed during colder seasons of less daylight. Emotionally, you may also experience a sense of isolation from the world. There can be a loss of direction, low energy levels, fatigue, and a tendency toward having a 'closed mind'. When your crown chakra is in balance, you will feel a sense of unity with others without suffering a loss of your individuality. You will pay well-focused attention to them. There is no distortion, but rather a knowledge born of wisdom or enlightenment. You will be free to follow your own ethical ideals and not be overly influenced by outside forces or the opinions of others.

Chakra	Balancing the Chakras - General	Meditation	Affirmation	Asanas
Muladhara	Get enough sleep every day and rest when you are tired. Massage is grounding and brings you back to body sensations. Foot massage is good. Eat regularly. Don't skip meals.	You can meditate using the seed mantra for this chakra, *Lam*.	A useful affirmation for this chakra is to repeat in your mind or out loud about 10 times, several times a day, "I stand firmly in my life in a loving and imaginative way".	All the standing postures help balance the root chakra. Tadasana Virabhadrasana I, II, III Utkatasana Garudasana Bhujangasana Salabhasana Marichyasana II Janu Sirasana Paschimottanasana Savasana
Svadhisthana	Massage can help you to let go of old emotions. Rolfing is a form of massage that can release memories from body tissue. It is deep and can be cathartic. But there are also gentler forms of massage that can release emotions for those who prefer a softer approach. Pranayama can help in letting go of emotions, especially with long exhalations.	You can meditate on the seed sound, *Vam*.	"I am open to the world and flow easily with changes in my life."	Trikonasana Pavritta Trikonasana Bhujangasana Salabhasana Dhanurasana Navasana Janu Sirasana Adha Badha Padma Paschimottanasana Baddha Konasana Paschimottanasana
Manipura	Jogging and powerwalking overcome sluggishness. Stomach crunches tone the area. Laughing or physical exercise help release suppressed emotions. Let go of emotional attachments that aren't helping you. Ask yourself what is running smoothly and enjoyably in your life right now. How can you use your will and less effort to achieve your goals?	You can meditate on empowerment or use the seed mantra, *Ram*.	"I move toward my goals smoothly and enjoyably."	Twists, back arches and forward stretches will assist the solar plexus chakra. Pavritta Trikonasana Marichyasana II Ustrasana Chakrasana Navasana Jathara Parivartanasana Paschimottanasana Purvottanasana Balasana
Anahata	An exercise to open the heart chakra is to sit in a crowded place. Choose a person to focus your mind on. While you sit relaxed and breathing deeply, take your time in observing their body movements, their face, their eyes and the way they speak. Put aside judgement. With each inhalation, build compassion for this person within you, but let go on each exhalation.	You can meditate on the seed mantra, *Yam*.	"My heart opens with love for all beings".	Virabhadrasana I Anjaneyasana Bhujangasana Matsyasana Ustrasana Urdva Dhanurasana Marichyasana II Passive opening out twist Balasana
Visuddha	Because this chakra operates on the level of vibration, chanting which works with the vibration of sound has a purifying effect. See the section on mantras (page 142). The breath can be used to calm the nervous system and enhance the quality of the voice, making it fuller, deeper and clearer. Practise Bhramari and Ujjayi breathing (see page 130).	You can meditate on the seed mantra, *Ham*, or chant it aloud.	"I communicate honestly and directly."	Salabhasana Bhujangasana Matsyasana Ustrasana Setu Bandhasana Sarvangasana Halasana Karnapidasana
Ajna	Meditation is key to opening the third eye chakra. Sit in a quiet place and focus on your breathing. Allow your breath to move to the area between and just above the eyebrows. Alternatively, do a color meditation, visualizing in turn each of the colors from the first to seventh chakra. From red, move through orange, yellow, green, blue, indigo and finally violet.	The seed sound for this chakra is *Om*.	"I am open to my inner guidance", or, 'I follow my inner guidance."	Matsyasana Setu bandhasana Sarvangasana Balasana Sirsasana Yogamudrasana
Sahasrara	To activate the crown chakra, live your life with as much awareness as possible. While this is more easily said than done, you can use breath awareness exercises, meditation, affirmation and asanas to help you.	Meditation taps into the world of the seventh chakra. There is no seed sound for this chakra, though you could chant the ancient sacred sound, *Om*.	"My soul is boundless and infinite."	Any meditation pose sitting erect with the back, neck and head in line is beneficial to working with the crown chakra. Sukhasana Siddhasana Vajarasana Balasana Sirsasana Sasankasana Yogamudrasana

Part 6

Therapeutic Yoga

Therapeutic Yoga

Yoga as a healing modality can be explained in two very different ways: Western and Eastern.

The Western Viewpoint

Physiologically, each yoga posture has specific structural and functional effects. By systematically placing pressure on the organs, the poses massage and help tone them. Adopting yoga postures, and flowing between them, opens and closes different areas of the body. Blood circulation improves and the lungs respond with a more efficient breath. Increased oxygen reaches the tissues, and every cell, tissue, organ and system reaps the benefits. As the stretching, flowing postures massage the lymphatic ducts, disposal of wastes is facilitated and becomes more efficient, the system is detoxified and the immune response enhanced. The body becomes physically stronger and excess tension is worked out of the system.

Many poses act on the endocrine glands by bathing them with fresh blood, which carries oxygen and vital nutrients to enhance overall functioning. Other postures and breathing techniques are believed to regulate the nervous system.

If you practice yoga asanas close to your edge, you can momentarily boost the sympathetic nervous system (involved in the "fight or flight" response) and therefore practice a safe, controlled way of responding to stress. When these poses are followed with poses that boost the parasympathetic nervous system, the "rest and repair" response is activated and the system is calmed and relaxed. The heartbeat slows, respiration steadies and blood pressure decreases. Levels of stress hormones decrease and healing mechanisms are turned on. In addition, when you become fully immersed in the sensations of the body, you take a mental holiday and become less preoccupied with the little worries of day-to-day life.

Relaxation techniques are considered deeply healing on many levels. Pranayama, like meditation, also has profound effects. Both assist the mental and emotional response of the person to their health condition, increasing the ability to detach from the disease and to identify, if only momentarily, with a higher level of existence. Yoga practice also tells us that the path is as important as the end result—a reminder to savour the journey through life, whatever it brings.

The Eastern Viewpoint

While Western doctors tend to treat the disease, traditional Eastern medicine treats the whole person. Western thought on disease is rather reductionist. Cellular dysfunction creates problems in tissues, which leads to dysfunction in the whole system.

The Eastern approach describes disease in a rather different way. Yoga is traditionally an individual practice where a teacher sees only one student as a time and therefore can work with them on a deeper level. Holistic medicine considers true health to lie far beyond the standard medical definition of "the absence of disease". Real health encompasses a state of supreme well-being and vitality on the physical, mental and spiritual levels. To be healthy, as the Sanskrit word for it—svastha—implies, is to be "established in yourself". When you have this solid basis, then you will also radiate joy and enthusiasm, which you experience as health. From the yogic viewpoint, Western treatments are often incomplete as medicine is prescribed on the basis of the symptoms and is not always intended to address the root cause; it cannot fully "cure" a patient.

Eastern thought considers more than just the physical, and takes into account five dimensions called koshas, or sheaths. Yoga seeks to harmonize each of the sheaths so that real cure can eventuate. The first dimension relates to the physical body. Organs, muscles, bones and all other tissues fall under this sheath, named the annamaya kosha. The second sheath incorporates the vital force and the essential physiological functions that keep our metabolism alive and healthy. It is known as the pranamaya kosha, and when the prana is disturbed, constrictions and blocks in the body and the breath will result. The third dimension is the manomaya kosha. Also called the astral sheath, or the body of will, it covers our mental and psychological state, incorporating mental abilities, thoughts, likes and dislikes, perceptions, cognition and knowledge gained by learning. Feelings like anger, depression and exhilaration are included and this kosha is linked to the subconscious mind. The fourth sheath, the vijnanamaya kosha, is referred to as the sheath of wisdom. It pertains to our body of knowledge, our deeper capacity to intuit the information gathered by the senses, the ability to trust and understand, to differentiate right from wrong, and to be able to see patterns from the past that still impact on our lives. When this sheath is perfectly healthy, all actions performed are in tune with cosmic laws. The final dimension, anandamaya kosha (spiritual sheath), refers to our spiritual selves. When the anandamaya kosha is perfectly healthy we have no illness at all, the ability to transcend misery and a sense of oneness and transcendence.

From the holistic viewpoint no one thing is independent of another. An imbalance in any one of the five sheaths can filter through to manifest symptoms in any of the others. When there are mental, emotional or pranic imbalances, the stress will tend to appear in the weakest organ of the physical body. This is how traditional Indian philosophy might explain any disease, be it a skin condition, heart disease or cancer. The more subtle the kosha, the greater its level of influence. The vital force (prana) affects the physical body more than changes in the body affect the prana. On the next level up in subtlety, the power of the mind, less dense than prana, will affect the prana and the physical body more than the other way around. This is why what we think is so important. The spirit, more subtle still, is the most powerful of all, and accounts for the strength of faith for healing and in experiencing perfect well-being.

Keeping the five sheaths in mind, we realize that at the same time as being physical beings, we are also mental, emotional and spiritual entities. We are multi-dimensional; none of these aspects can be ignored. With this in mind, it is possible to be a wonderful, complete and healthy person (on the mental, emotional and spiritual levels) who also happens to carry a (physical level) disease. While it seems like two opposing thoughts, it is possible to experience the feeling of wholeness while holding the knowledge of illness in the mind at the same time. Under this dual reality, it is possible to experience a wonderful sense of well-being even should the physical body be dying.

Therapeutic yoga has practices to cover each of the sheaths. To work more specifically with the annamaya (physical) kosha, asanas and yogic kriyas (cleansing practices), and good diet are essential practices. Pranayama and yogic cleansing practices work on the level of the pranamaya (energy) kosha. For the manomaya (will) and vijnanamaya (wisdom) koshas, analysis, learning, experience, meditation and the devotional aspects of yoga, such as the chanting of mantras, are used. To benefit the anandamaya (bliss) kosha one can practice relaxation, meditation and tuning into the experience of bliss.

Introduction to the table of conditions

Yoga aims to treat the individual, not just their disease. With this in mind, it is recommended you see a yoga therapist or an experienced teacher. In holistic medicine there are no set "recipes" for the treatment of any disease. However, this table may act as a guide to the sort of postures that have been known to help various health conditions. For any health condition, seeing a natural medicine practitioner is a great investment. They can help you identify the cause of your illness and you may be surprised by how many niggling health complaints tie in with your main concerns and can also be treated.

Pose	AIDS	Anxiety	Arthritis	Asthma	Back Pain	Cancer
Healing Visualisation	★		✓	✓	✓	
Meditation	★	★	✓	★	✓	
Nadi Suddhi	★	★	✓	✓	✓	
Ujjayi Breathing			✓	★	✓	
Bhramari Breathing	★	★	✓	✓	✓	
Viparita Karani	✓				✓	
Chair Yoga	✓		✓			
Restorative Yoga	✓		✓	✓	✓	
Surya Namaskar	✓		✓	✓		
Halasana	✓	★			✓	
Sarvangasana	✓	★		✓		
Sirsasana	✓			✓		
Bhujapidasana & Bakasana		✓				
Navasana		✓			★	
Passive Reclining Twist	✓	✓			✓	
Passive Opening Out Twist	✓		✓	✓		
Jathara Parivartanasana		✓			✓	
Marichyasana III	✓				✓	
Pavritta Sukhasana	✓	✓	✓		✓	
Chakrasana		✓		✓		
Matsyasana	✓			✓		
Setu Bandhasana	✓	✓	✓	★	✓	
Salabhasana		✓		★	✓	
Bhujangasana	✓	✓	✓	★	✓	
Upavista Konasana			✓		✓	
Baddha Konasana						
Purvottanasana		✓		✓		
Paschimottanasana	✓		✓	✓	✓	✓
Janu Sirsasana	✓			✓	✓	✓
Standing Postures		✓	✓		✓	
Awareness of the Breath		✓	✓	★		
Roll Downs		★		✓	✓	
Biralasana	✓	✓	✓	★	✓	
Discovering the Breath	✓	★	✓		✓	
Savasana Relaxation	✓	★		✓	✓	

Key

✓ Recommended

★ Key Pose

✕ Not Recommended

AIDS—Sarvangasana assists immune system by stimulating lymphatic drainage. Refer to the entries for cancer and immune support.

Anxiety—Practice conscious breathing throughout the day to shift your thoughts away from concerns and bring you back to the present moment. Physically work stress out with the asanas and perform them with as much mental focus as possible. After asana work, release in Savasana.

Arthritis—Practice joint-limbering movements first of all. If it is difficult to hold a pose, don't stay in it for long. Instead, develop mobility in the joints by moving in and out of the pose with easy flowing movements. Use props where necessary.

Asthma—It is possible to cure asthma with yoga. Backbends are useful as they lift and open the chest, encouraging fuller breathing. Take care not to collapse the chest in while practicing forward bends. Pranayama practices will retrain the breath and develop a longer exhalation.

Back Pain—It is essential to get a correct diagnosis and is then best to work with an experienced teacher and what is appropriate for your condition. Start with gentle standing postures and breath work. Then introduce backbends, twists and forward bends.

Cancer—Maintain a low-chemical, low-stress lifestyle and aim to nourish yourself with yoga practise so that you will be more naturally drawn to a

Condition	30	128	37	38	36	40	61	63	69	65	64	76	75	78	79	000	84	89	86	88	86	95	86	96	102	104	106	109	110	116	113	130	131	132	136	33
stimulate the digestive system and encourage elimination. Rehydrate well before and after yoga practice.			✓						✓									✓		✓		✓							✓			✓	✓	✓	✓	✓
Depression—To help stay in the present moment, keep the eyes open during asana practice. Avoid long holding of forward bends as they tend to make you more introspective.		★					★	★	✗			★	★	★	★	★	★	✓	★	✓	★	✓		✓	★	★	★	★	✓	✓	✓	✓	✓	✓	★	✓
Diabetes—Twists and backbends tone the pancreas. Yoga asanas in general support the nervous system, increase circulation and improve overall vitality.			✓	✓	✓	✓	✓	✓			✓	✓	✓	✓	✓		✓	✓	✓	★		✓			✓				✓		✓	✓	✓	✓	✓	✓
Elderly People—Although the poses might not be as extended as those in the photographs, performing them with awareness will bring the same benefits. Flow into and out of poses, rather than holding them. Use props where necessary. The breath work and relaxation are always necessary.			✓	✓	✓	✓	✓				✓	✓	✓	✓					★	✓		✓			✓				✓	✓	★		✓	✓		
Enlarged Prostate—Supta Konasana, which brings vitality to the pelvic area, and Viparita Karani may help relieve minor blockages.			✓	✓	✓		✓																		✓					✓						
Fatigue—Consult a health professional to find the cause, especially for the sudden onset of fatigue. Surya Namaskar revives mental alertness. Inversions help clear the mind. Restore with forward bends and Savasana. Re-energise with pranayama.	✓				✓	✓		✓		✓				✓				✓				✓							✓	★			✓			✓
Fever—Yoga asanas shouldn't be practiced with a fever. The pranayama exercises in this book can increase heat in the body so they should be avoided. Practice relaxation and healing visualization until you are over your illness and resume asana practice with restorative poses.	✓																			✓																
Herniated (Slipped) Spinal Disc—Yoga can effectively manage slipped discs. Forward bending should be avoided initially as the affected area of the back needs to be kept concave while bending forward. Use abdominal strengtheners and backbends initially, allowing 24 hours for body feedback.	★											★	★	★	★	★			★	✓			★							✓	★	✓		★	★	★
Hypertension—The aerobic effect of Surya Namaskar dilates the blood vessels, which lowers blood pressure. However, if your blood pressure is very high, it is best to keep the head above the heart. Practice relaxation, pranayama and meditation. Avoid holding the breath.	★													✗	✗		✗								✗											
Immune Support—After asana practice, take extra time for Savasana and for pranayama. While asana practice encourages health on the cellular level, Savasana greatly assists healing on a deep level. Pranayama calms the mind and relieves the stress associated with chronic illness.	✓														✓	✓	✓	✓	✓	✓	✓	✓	✓		✓			✓	✓	✓	✓	✓	✓	✓	✓	✓
Insomnia—Both mind and body rest more easily after being extended. Do energizing asanas like Surya Namaskar and backbends in the mornings. If your practice is closer to bedtime, focus on forward bends and inversions. Before bed, practice Nadi Suddhi and meditation.	✓																											★	★	★		★	✓	✓	★	
Menstrual Disorders—Backbends, forward bends, twists and Surya Namaskar increase vitality to the pelvic area. Supta Konasana and Halasana/Supported Halasana are key poses. Inverted postures help in balancing hormones.								✓	✓	✓	★	✓										✓							★	★	★					
Menstruation—Inversions, strong twists and strong backbends should not be practiced during menstruation. Forward bends are recommended during this time. Practice poses from the restorative sequence, except for supported Plough.												✓	✓	✗	✗		✗								✗	✗	✗	✗	★	★	★					
Neck Pain—If the cause is tension, arm balances and bhujangasana help work the muscles so they can subsequently relax. Don't hunch the shoulders in standing poses, nor round them in forward bends. Never over-stretch the neck in twists. Avoid Headstand, Shoulderstand and Plough.											✓		✓	✓										✓	✗	✗	✗									
Obesity—Sun Salutation will help burn energy. Practice plenty of standing poses, backbends and inversions. If you over-eat because of emotional factors, maintain a regular asana practice and include pranayama exercises and meditation.	✓	✓	✓	✓	✓	✓	✓	✓	✓	✓	✓	✓	✓	✓	✓	✓	✓	✓	✓	✓		✓		✓	✓	✓			✓	✓	✓	✓		✓	✓	✓
Pregnancy—To increase your enjoyment of this special time, attend prenatal classes. Do not begin yoga asanas in the first trimester. As the ligaments soften in pregnancy, take care not to overstretch. Rather than holding the postures for a long time, enjoy flowing into and out of them.	★						★																							✓	✓			✓		✓
Stress—Some mental stress can be physically worked out in the asanas. Concentrating on body awareness during asana practice gives a mental break from worrying about other things. Long Savasana releases mental and physical tension. Pranayama calms the nervous system.	✓	✓	✓	✓	✓	✓	✓	✓	✓	✓	✓	✓	✓	✓	✓	✓	✓	✓	✓	✓	✓	✓	✓	✓	✓	✓	✓	✓	✓	✓	✓	✓	✓	✓	✓	✓
Varicose Veins—Get clearance from your doctor that you have no existing blood clots that may be dislodged. Stimulate the circulation with Surya Namaskar. Include Shoulderstand or Viparita Karani in your practice.																									★			★			★					

For reference see page

abhyasa 11
Adho Mukha Svanasana 100–1
ahimsa 18
AIDS 158
ajna (third eye) chakra 151–2, 153
Alternate Nostril Breathing 132–3
anahata (heart) chakra 150, 153
Anjaneyasana 74
anxiety 158
aparigraha 19–20
Ardha Baddha Padma
  Paschimottanasana 62
Arm Pressure Balance 96
arthritis 158
asanas 10–12, 13, 21
asteya 19
asthma 158

back pain 158
backbends 70–81
  chair exercise 116
Baddha Konasana 65
Bakasana 97
balances 90–7
Balasana 28, 29, 81
bandhas 15, 138
Bhagavad-Gita 21
Bhajrava Mudra 138
Bhakti Yoga 143
Bharadvajasana I 85
Bhramari 130
Bhujangasana 76
Bhujapidasana 96
Biralasana 37
Boat Pose 95
Bound Angle Pose 65
Bound Half Lotus Forward Fold 62
brahmacharya 19
breath 12, 21, 34–5, 124–5
  Awareness of the Breath 36
  Discovering the Breath 128–9
  see also pranayama
breathing bed 32
Breathing in All Directions 128–9
Bridge Pose 78

Camel Pose 77
cancer 158
Cat Pose 37
centering 116
chair exercises 116–17
chakra meditation 140
chakras 146–53
chanting 143
Chest Opening Exercise 36
Chest to Leg Extension 52
Child Pose 28, 29, 81
classes 25
clothing 24
Cobbler's Pose 65
Cobra Pose 76
color visualization 33
constipation 159
Corpse Pose (Savasana) 27, 30–1
  Variation 69
Cow Face Pose 68
Crane Pose 97
Crescent Moon Pose 74
Crocodile Pose (Makrasana) 28, 114
Cross-Legged Forward Fold 39

Cross-Legged Twist 84
crown (sahasrara) chakra 152, 153

Dandasana 58
depression 27, 54, 159
dharana 21, 140
dhyana 21
diabetes 159
discomfort 15–16
Downward-Facing Dog 100–1

Eagle Pose 93
edges 16
elderly people 116, 159
enlarged prostate 159
evening sessions 120–1

fatigue 159
fever 159
Fish Pose 79
five sheaths 157–8
forward bends 54–69
  Forward Bend with a Chair 112
  seated 117

Garudasana 93
Gomukhasana 68
Gyana Mudra 138

Halasana 106
Hand to Foot Pose 92
Hare Pose 102, 103
Hatha Yoga Pradipika 21, 125
Head Beyond The Knee Pose
  (Janu Sirsasana) 61, 81
Headstand 102–3
healing visualization 33
heart (anahata) chakra 150, 153
Hero Pose 59
Humming Bee Breath 130
hypertension 54, 71, 159

immune support 159
insomnia 159
Intense Forward Stretch 50–1
inversions 98–107
ishvarapranidhana 21

Janu Sirsasana 61, 81
Jathara Parivartanasana 86–7

Karnapidasana 107
Knee to Ear Pose 107
koshas 157–8
kundalini path 146–7

Locust Pose 75

Makrasana 28, 114
manipura (solar plexus) chakra
  149–50, 153
mantras 142–3
Marichyasana III 89
mats 24
Matsyasana 79
meditation 21, 136–41
menstruation 25, 54, 71, 83, 99, 110, 159
Mighty Pose 46
morning sessions 118–19
Mountain Pose 43

moving meditation 140
Mudras 138
mulabandha 15
muladhara (root) chakra 147–8, 153

Nadi Suddhi Pranayama 132–3
nadis 146
Navasana 95
neck pain 159
niyamas 20–1

obesity 159

pain 15–16
palming 117
Parsvakonasana 45
Parsvottanasana 52
Paschimottanasana 63, 81
Passive Opening Out Twist 88
Passive Reclining Twist 81
Pavritta Sukhasana 84
Pavritta Trikonasana 53
pillows 28
Plough Pose 106
practice
  basic guidelines 24–5
  structuring 118–21
prana 11, 124, 157
pranayama 21, 124–33
Prasarita Padottanasana 49
pratyahara 21
pregnancy 25, 71, 83, 92, 99, 159
Purvottanasana 69

Reclining Big Toe Pose 66–7
Reclining Hero Pose 73
relaxation 26–33
Restorative Inversion
  (Viparita Karani) 28, 113
restorative poses 110–15
Revitalising Relaxation 32
Revolved Abdomen Pose 86–7
Revolved Triangle Pose 53
Rocking 81
Roll Downs 38
root (muladhara) chakra 147–8, 153

Sage Twist I 85
Sage Twist III 89
sahasrara (crown) chakra 152, 153
Salabhasana 75
Salamba Halasana 115
samadhi 21
santosha 20
Sarvangasana 104–5
Sasankasana 102, 103
satya 18–19
saucha 20
Savasana 27, 30–1
  Variation 69
Sealing Pose (Yogamudrasana) 81, 138
Seated Wide Angle Pose Sequence 64
Setu Bandhasana 78
sexual (svadhisthana) chakra 148–9, 153
Shoulderstand 104–5
Siddhasana 127
Side Angle Stretch 45
Sirsasana 102–3
sitting positions 127
slipped disc 159

solar plexus (manipura) chakra
  149–50, 153
Staff Pose 58
standing postures 40–53
stress 159
Stretch on the East Side of the Body 69
Stretch on the West Side of the Body
  (Paschimottanasana) 63, 81
structuring practice 118–21
Sukhasana 127
Sukhasana Forward Fold 39
Sukhasana Twist 81
Sun Salutation 108–9
Supported Angle Pose
  (Supta Konasana) 28, 111
Supported Plough Pose 115
Supta Konasana 28, 111
Supta Padangustasana 66–7
Supta Virasana 73
Surya Namaskar 108–9
svadhisthana (sexual) chakra 148–9, 153
swadhyaya 20–1

Tadasana 43
tapas 20
therapeutic yoga 156–9
third eye (ajna) chakra 151–2, 153
Three Limbed Forward Bend 60
throat (visuddha) chakra 151, 153
time 24–5
trataka 140
Trianga Mukhaikapada
  Paschimottanasana 60
Triangle Pose 48
Trikonasana 48
twists 82–9
  chair exercise 117

uddhyanabandha 15
Ujjayi Pranayama 131
Upavista Konasana 64
Upward Facing Bow Pose 80
Urdva Dhanurasana 80
Ustrasana 77
Utkatasana 46
Uttanasana 50–1
Utthita Hasta Padangusthasana 92

Vajarasana 127
varicose veins 159
Victorious Breath 131
Viparita Karani 28, 113
Virabhadrasana I 47
Virabhadrasana II 44
Virabhadrasana III 94
Virasana 59
visualization 33
visuddha (throat) chakra 151, 153

Warrior I 47
Warrior II 44
Warrior III 94
Wide Leg Stretch 49

yamas 18–20
yoga nidra 26
Yoga-Sutra 11–12, 13, 18, 21
Yogamudrasana 81, 138

Z Pose 69